Pray & Go

TYNDALE
MOMENTUM®

A Tyndale nonfiction imprint

PRAY
& G⊙

A 30-DAY JOURNEY

Your Invitation to Become a
Great Commission Christian

THOM S. RAINER

Visit Tyndale online at tyndale.com.

Visit Tyndale Momentum online at tyndalemomentum.com.

Tyndale, Tyndale's quill logo, *Tyndale Momentum*, and the Tyndale Momentum logo are registered trademarks of Tyndale House Ministries. Tyndale Momentum is a nonfiction imprint of Tyndale House Publishers, Carol Stream, Illinois.

Pray & Go: Your Invitation to Become a Great Commission Christian

Designed by Sarah Susan Richardson

Some names have been changed for the privacy of individuals.

All Scripture quotations are taken from the *Holy Bible*, New Living Translation, copyright © 1996, 2004, 2015 by Tyndale House Foundation. Used by permission of Tyndale House Publishers, Carol Stream, Illinois 60188. All rights reserved.

For information about special discounts for bulk purchases, please contact Tyndale House Publishers at csresponse@tyndale.com, or call 1-855-277-9400.

Library of Congress Cataloging-in-Publication Data

A catalog record for this book is available from the Library of Congress.

ISBN 978-1-4964-4905-4

Printed in China

29	28	27	26	25	24	23
7	6	5	4	3	2	1

To

Canon Rainer,

my first grandson.

You make me incredibly proud,

and I love you very much.

And always to

Nellie Jo,

the greatest Great Commission Christian I know.

CONTENTS

INTRODUCTION

YOU'VE TAKEN A GIANT STEP

Thank you for opening to the first pages of this book. I mean it with all my heart. Thank you.

At the very least, you're curious about what it means to become a Great Commission Christian.

Here's my promise to you: If you will read every chapter, representing thirty days of a Great Commission focus, I have no doubt you will become an instrument of outreach and ministry for God in new and powerful ways.

God does not intend for us to keep the Good News to ourselves. We are meant to share our faith, to tell others about what God has done in our lives through Jesus Christ.

God also designed us for community—that is, to be connected to other believers through the local church. From Acts

2 to Revelation 3, the New Testament is all about the local church. It is the story of local churches making a difference in the world. It is the story of messy and messed-up churches still being used by God. It is the story of sinners like you and me being saved by grace. It is the story of God giving us a second chance again and again.

You see, God designed us to be bearers of the truth about his son, Jesus. And he intends for us to carry out the Great Commission mostly in the context of a local church.

If you are a church member, you are a bearer of the Good News. Well, you *should* be a bearer of the Good News.

At Church Answers, our team continues to look at information coming from the front lines of ministry called the local church. We have provided a tool called Know Your Church that helps churches and church members self-evaluate. We look at six areas of church life: *evangelism*, *discipleship*, *prayer*, *ministry*, *fellowship*, and *worship*. Do you know which one consistently scores the lowest? If you guessed *evangelism*, you are correct.

SATAN AND EVANGELISM

The gospel of Jesus Christ is about truth. Jesus himself said, "I am the way, the truth, and the life. No one can come to the Father except through me" (John 14:6). Paul wrote to the church at Corinth: "[Love] does not rejoice about injustice but rejoices whenever the truth wins out" (1 Corinthians 13:6). The truth of the gospel is meant to be shared. The way of salvation through Christ is meant to be on the lips of believers.

But Satan will do everything within his great, but limited, power to keep the truth of the gospel from spreading. Speaking of the devil, Jesus said, "He was a murderer from the beginning. He has always hated the truth, because there is no truth in him. When he lies, it is consistent with his character; for he is a liar and the father of lies" (John 8:44).

Simply stated, the father of lies does not want us sharing the truth. Sadly, at least in the North American context, we often see Satan winning these battles in our churches. He has given us a bevy of lies to keep us silent.

"I don't have time."

"I don't want to offend people."

"I might get rejected."

"Evangelism is not my spiritual gift."

"That's what we pay the pastor to do."

"I don't need to *talk* about Jesus; I'll just *show* my love to others."

THE NEW TESTAMENT CHRISTIAN AND EVANGELISM

Peter and John were in jail. Their crime? Telling people about Jesus. The authorities gave the two apostles a way out. If they promised to stop talking about their Savior, they would be set free. The conditions were clear: "They called the apostles back in and commanded them never again to speak or teach in the name of Jesus" (Acts 4:18).

It could have been a life-and-death situation. If the apostles promised to stop talking about Jesus to unbelievers, they would be set free. If not, they would be punished. They might get long prison sentences. They might get flogged with a whip. Or they might face execution.

Faced with these dire possibilities, Peter and John did not hesitate to respond: "Do you think God wants us to obey you rather than him? We cannot stop telling about everything we have seen and heard" (Acts 4:19-20).

Ironic, isn't it? Faced with possible death, Peter and John continued to tell others about Jesus. Today, many church members remain silent lest they offend someone or inconvenience themselves.

A PLAN TO JUMP-START YOUR OUTWARD FOCUS

When I was a young seminary student, I had little time and little money. The last thing I needed was an ornery car that wouldn't start. But my car was totally stubborn. Sometimes it wouldn't start in the mornings. Sometimes it went dead during the day. On a few occasions, it died while I was in traffic.

I finally joined AAA so I wouldn't have to pay for the

jump-starting service every time the car quit on me—which was typically two or three times a month. I didn't have the funds to get it repaired or even to buy a new battery.

For a few years, I saw the power of jump-starting. The AAA service person would connect the cables to his truck and then to my car. My automobile came to life every time.

I've needed spiritual jump-starting on many occasions. I certainly needed jump-starting to restore a Great Commission focus. This book is designed to provide you with a Great Commission jump-start. It focuses on three main areas: *prayer*, *Scripture*, and *going out*.

A PLAN FOR YOUR CHURCH

At Church Answers, we have designed a program we call Pray & Go to help church members develop an outward focus, get out into their communities, pray for their neighbors and their cities, and invite people to church.[1] This book incorporates many of the same principles into a thirty-day action plan that any church member or group can implement.

Ideally, several members of your church will embark on this adventure with you. You will pray together. You will encourage one another. You will hold each other accountable.

Yes, you can move through the thirty days of this book on your own. But the better scenario is for several members to move forward together. In 1 Corinthians 12:12-27, Paul refers to the local church as *the body of Christ*. We are all different members of the body (which is why we are called church members). Each member of the body—the metaphorical hand, foot, ear, eye—must function well and properly for the entire body to function as intended.

Would you make a commitment right now to go through each of the thirty days in this book? The process isn't designed to be cumbersome or time-consuming, but it is designed to be completed.

Once you have completed the thirty days, you will have taken fifteen days to pray about becoming outwardly focused. You will have studied five key Bible passages about reaching beyond yourself to others. You will have prayed in front of sixty homes in your community. You will have sent a note or email to five people who are not part of your church. And you will have specifically invited eight people to visit your church.

That's all in a very achievable thirty days—thirty days that can change your life and the life of your community.

That's if you do it alone.

But if *ten* people from your church will commit to these thirty days of Great Commission focus, together you will invest 150 days of prayer toward developing an outward focus for your church. Together, you will study what the Bible says about the Great Commission for a total of fifty days. You will write to forty people and invite eighty people to church. And you will have gone out into your community and prayed for six hundred families and their homes.

Ten's not that many, so what about twenty-five?

Here are the totals from a simple thirty-day commitment to becoming Great Commission Christians:

- 375 days of prayer to recalibrate your church to an outward focus.
- 125 days of studying what the Scriptures say about the Great Commission.
- 125 notes or emails to people and 200 invitations to church.
- And you will have gone into your community and prayed for 1,500 families and their homes!

In God's power, you can change the world. You can turn it upside down. And if a few other members of your church join you, you will have a Great Commission *movement* in your community.

Are you ready to make a commitment that will change your life in exciting and powerful ways? Are you ready—in God's power—to change the world?

If you are willing, please sign the commitment below. It's a way to make you accountable to God and to yourself.

Now get ready for a great adventure!

As God guides and enables me, I commit to move forward with the thirty-day plan to become a Great Commission Christian.

Name: ....

Date: ....

PRAYING FOR A HEART WITH AN OUTWARD FOCUS

The first church that I served as pastor was on the cusp of closing. One of the seven remaining members clearly communicated to me that the church was at a critical juncture. Would they call the new, young pastor, or would they admit that it was time to close down the church? After she heard me preach, she had all but decided that the doors needed to close.

"We have had some bad preachers," she said bluntly, "but you're probably the worst I've ever heard. It's a toss-up to me whether we close the doors or have to listen to you every week."

Sigh.

So much for encouragement from your membership.

The church had been around since the late 1700s, coming together just a few years after our nation was founded. It had served a rural farming community well for two centuries. But most of the farmers were gone now. The community had no businesses to speak of. It didn't even have a traffic light. The situation was bleak.

Within a few weeks, I learned that the church had called me as pastor because they had no other candidates. Again, not very encouraging.

I am not the hero of this story, but it is a good story. God gave me the opportunity to share the gospel with someone. That one person became God's instrument to reach others. One by one, our few church members decided they did not want to close the doors after all. One by one, they started reaching outward instead of being inwardly focused.

We had no musicians in the church except our piano player. She hit the right note about half the time. When the congregation sang along, we barely made a joyful noise. The facilities were in disrepair. There were no restrooms, only an abandoned outhouse that reportedly was home to several snakes. I never checked it out.

We had only a few hundred dollars in the bank, enough to pay my weekly salary of fifty dollars, but with not much left for ministry. Our members were understandably discouraged.

But God had a plan for our church . . .

Instead of dying, it began to thrive. Instead of giving in to discouragement, our members became bearers of encouragement. Instead of bemoaning our paucity of resources, they grew in faith that God would provide us and the church everything we needed.

It didn't happen overnight, but our members started talking to other people in the rural community. They expanded their conversations to people in two adjacent communities. They developed an amazing commitment to prayer. Simply stated, they prayed for hearts with an outward focus. They prayed that God would use them to reach people. They prayed they would be God's instruments to fulfill the Great Commission.

God heard. God answered.

Over the next several years, the church reached many people with the gospel, growing in both numbers and depth of discipleship. They were still reaching and discipling people years after I left.

PRAYING FOR YOURSELF

I would guess that you have prayed for your own needs many times. My own prayer life has included prayers to be a better dad and husband. I have three incredible sons and a wife who is a gift from God. Though I know I don't deserve them, I love them dearly. I have messed up in both my roles—as dad and husband. I have prayed prayers of repentance for my bouts of selfishness, anger, inattentiveness, and indifference. I have needed to ask God to help me get my act together.

Now in the autumn of my life, I pray also for my eleven grandchildren. I pray that I would be a godly granddad (or "Rad Rad," as they call me), that God would make me a good example and a joy to my family.

I know you have prayed for yourself as well. Perhaps you identify with some of my prayers. Perhaps you have prayed for spiritual healing, physical healing, or emotional healing. One of the greatest prayers you can pray for yourself is to become a Great Commission Christian—outwardly focused on advancing the gospel.

PRAYING FOR YOURSELF TO BECOME A GREAT COMMISSION CHRISTIAN

I will use the phrase *Great Commission Christian* from time to time in this book. There are several passages of Scripture where Jesus commands us to share the Good News and go and make disciples. Perhaps the best-known passage is Matthew 28:18-20: "Jesus came and told his disciples, 'I have been given all authority in heaven and on earth. Therefore, go and make disciples of all the nations, baptizing them in the name of the Father and the Son and the Holy Spirit. Teach these new disciples to obey all the commands I have given you. And be sure of this: I am with you always, even to the end of the age.'"

We will study that passage more closely on Day 19. For now, we will use the basic understanding that the Great Commission is all about sharing the gospel of Christ with unbelievers and then helping those who commit their lives to Christ to grow as his disciples. Simply stated, a Great Commission Christian is someone who seeks to communicate the Good News of Christ to a world that does not know him.

On this first day of the thirty-day challenge, please pray for yourself. Pray specifically that God will use you in supernatural ways over the next month. Here are some suggestions on areas for prayer:

- For a heart that prioritizes reaching others with the gospel.
- For open opportunities to share the gospel and invite people to church.
- For good time management—to not be so busy that you can't do the work God has called you to do.
- To be an encourager for others in your church to become Great Commission Christians as well.
- To have the right words to say, or not to say, when you have the opportunity to share the gospel or invite someone to church.

- To be the type of servant to others that causes them to be drawn to the Savior who works through you.

You are praying that God will make you a consistent Great Commission Christian. You want your heart to be receptive and your eyes to be open to the world as Christ sees the world.

TIME TO PRAY

Day 1 is a day of prayer. Day 1 is a day of commitment. Day 1 is the beginning of your great adventure.

On fourteen of the next thirty days, you will be asked to do nothing other than pray. That's because prayer is *essential* to your becoming a Great Commission Christian. If you try to accomplish this goal in your own power, you will not succeed. If you seek God's direction and power, you will see victories in your life, in the lives of others, and in your church.

So it's time to pray. You will have other days to pray about other important matters, but this day is a time for you to pray for yourself. You can use the guide above, and of course you can pray any way you feel led.

Would you pray now for a Great Commission heart with an outward focus?

Sign and date here when you have completed the first day of the thirty-day challenge to become a Great Commission Christian.

Name: ....

Date: ....

YOU *WILL* BE MY WITNESSES

Raising three sons was an adventure. They are now grown and have given my wife and me eleven grandchildren—as I'm prone to mention from time to time. Growing up, the boys were good kids, but like any other kids, they could be incredibly sweet and incredibly stubborn.

It was one of those nights when we were all worn out. The boys had had a full day at school followed by sports in the afternoon. Typically, when they came home, they wanted a bit of a break before beginning their schoolwork. Nellie Jo and I tried to be understanding, but there were only so many hours in a day. The homework had to be done.

Like other kids their age, our sons often found a screen to entertain themselves. Whether it was a video game or old-fashioned television, they enjoyed their few minutes of respite. They knew that the moment they heard their mom call, "Supper is ready," the joy in their lives would come to a screeching halt. And yes, my Southern bride calls it *supper*, not *dinner*.

The call to supper meant that screen time was over. After our meal, there would be a shower, homework, and bed. The latter three items were not part of the boys' fun routines.

When Nellie Jo called the first time, two of our sons dutifully came to the supper table. One son, whose name will not be mentioned, could not pull himself away. Nellie Jo called again, this time using his first and last name before exclaiming again, "Supper is ready!"

There was still no response. The two brothers at the table looked down. I couldn't tell if they were smiling in anticipation of or simply avoiding the fireworks to come.

This time Nellie Jo left the dining area. She proceeded with authority to the prodigal son's bedroom, where he was still transfixed to a screen. This time the decibels decidedly increased. It was no longer his first and last name; it was his first, middle, and last name. Then came the declaration: "You *will* come to supper."

Her emphasis on the word *will* made it crystal clear that Nellie Jo was not making a request; she was issuing a command.

You may be curious to know what happened if one of the

boys did not obey the third call. I don't know. None of them had the temerity to find out.

WHEN JESUS SAYS "WILL"

Let's look at Acts 1:8: "You will receive power when the Holy Spirit comes upon you. And you will be my witnesses, telling people about me everywhere—in Jerusalem, throughout Judea, in Samaria, and to the ends of the earth."

There it is again: "You *will.*" There is no second option. There is either obedience or disobedience. You will be his witnesses, or you will be disobedient to your Savior. It is a command, not a request.

On the first day of this thirty-day challenge, you committed to ask God to change your heart so you can become more focused on the Great Commission, on being the witness that Christ has called you to be. Let's take a moment, then, and unpack this important verse.

START WITH THE SOURCE OF THE POWER

If you had asked me what my greatest fear was early in my adult life, the answer would have been easy. I feared speaking in public. In fact, when I was a businessman involved in a local church, I made sure I arrived at my Sunday school class a few minutes late. I wanted to avoid the opening prayer time lest someone call on me. Seriously.

When it became clear that I was called to vocational ministry, my wife and I stared at each other for a few minutes. I asked her how I could be in ministry if I couldn't speak in public. She didn't have an answer.

But God had the answer.

He has given me everything I've needed to fulfill his call on my life. As I look back over forty years of ministry, I am amazed at how incredibly well God has taken care of me. I have spoken in all fifty states and many different countries.

If you have any hesitation about this thirty-day challenge, remember that you are not going it alone. You *will* receive power. In fact, I think you will be amazed by how God will change you in such a brief period.

MAKING THE "WILL" THE "WANT"

As you receive the power of the Holy Spirit, the command to be witnesses will seem less a task to be completed as a joy to be shared. You will *want* to be a witness for Christ. You will see Acts 1:8 as a joy to be completed rather than a command to be obeyed.

Keep in mind, these were Jesus' last words before he ascended to heaven. Like a last will and testament, his words had significant import. They were the last words he would speak on earth until we see him face-to-face. He has asked us to do this one thing. Be a witness for him. Tell others about him.

START WHERE YOU ARE

Jesus' command in Acts 1:8 begins with Jerusalem, where his disciples were at the time. In other words, we are to start by being witnesses right where we are. We don't have to wait for some spectacular revelation from God. We will hear from him even more clearly as we obey his command to share the gospel in our local community.

I had a phone conversation with my middle son, Art, and he offered some powerful insight. He said, "You know, Dad, I have discovered that I rarely hear from God when I'm sitting around doing nothing. That just doesn't seem to be the way he wants me to wait on him. I hear from him clearly, though, when I'm doing something for him. It might be as simple as being kind to a server or inviting someone to church. I hear from God when I'm *doing*. That's the best kind of waiting."

He's right. The purpose of these thirty days is to get you to do something outwardly, to look beyond yourself. Where do you begin? Right where you are. Right in your own Jerusalem.

READ, THINK, PRAY, READ AGAIN

Your assignment today is simple. Read Acts 1:8. Think about Jesus' words. Think about how those words to his disciples apply to you today. Pray about the passage. Ask God to make it come alive in your life.

Then read it again. And perhaps a third time.

Ask God to show you how to be a Jerusalem witness. He may give you opportunities to witness beyond Jerusalem, but that's where you begin, right where you are.

You are about to have an exciting new world open up to you because you have chosen to be obedient where you are. This verse is foundational for your thirty days. Though we will deal with other verses as we go along, you might decide to come back to this second day to get your marching orders.

Moreover, you might need to be reminded that the power to move forward on your journey is not your own: "You will receive power when the Holy Spirit comes upon you."

Day 2 is done. Tomorrow we will explore how to become an instrument to pray for your church.

Sign and date here when you have completed the second day of the thirty-day challenge to become a Great Commission Christian.

Name: ....

Date: ....

GETTING THE BODY MOVING

Though I don't enjoy going to the doctor, I absolutely love and trust my doctor. He has been my primary care physician for almost two decades. He is a strong Christian, a good friend, and an incredible internist. I have rarely seen anyone in any field with his insights.

He is a deep-thinking researcher on medical issues. I can count on him to have read and absorbed many volumes of medical advancements and discoveries. Recently, he shared with me some amazing research about mobility and health. He told me that taking a few thousand steps a day is instrumental to good health and longevity. He encouraged me to walk at least ten thousand steps a day.

"The human body is meant to move, Thom," my doctor

told me. "When we get sedentary, we are more likely to have all kinds of physical problems."

We must get our bodies moving.

As a result, I use a smartphone app to measure my steps every day. I don't always get to ten thousand, but sometimes I go over significantly.

GETTING THE BODY (OF CHRIST) MOVING

There are several metaphors for the church in Scripture, but my favorite is "the body of Christ." And my favorite specific passage is 1 Corinthians 12:12-27.

Let's take a quick look at the background of the church at Corinth, the recipient of the apostle Paul's letter. The city itself was largely affluent. It was the capital of a Roman province. It had a favorable geography, and it was an influential city in the Roman Empire.

Sadly, the church at Corinth reflected the culture of the city instead of influencing it. There were lawsuits among the church members. Paul clearly said that such lawsuits were prohibited. There were no exception clauses. The church at Corinth had to deal with sexual immorality, abuse of spiritual gifts, and abuse of Christian freedoms that hurt the witness of the believers in the church.

Paul traveled to Corinth on his second missionary journey and spent about eighteen months there. He knew the city well. He knew the church well. And, of course, he knew the church well. While Paul mandated several corrective actions in the church, he also reminded the members poignantly of how they were supposed to function.

Metaphorically, each member is like a member of the human body. Paul makes it clear that "the human body has many parts, but the many parts make up one whole body" (1 Corinthians 12:12). Each of those parts or members is designed to function, whether it is a "foot," a "hand," an "eye," or an "ear." In simple terms, they were designed to do something. They were not designed for a sedentary life.

Like my doctor told me, movement means health and longevity. Similarly, movement in your church means greater health for the congregation as well.

PRAYING TO GET YOUR CHURCH MOVING

First, I want to make it clear not to wait for others before you commit to moving forward for your church. You are courageous to participate in this thirty-day challenge regardless of what others do. This commitment is first between you and God.

I also want to be clear that the healthiest churches are those where *several* members are moving forward with a Great Commission focus. I've had the joy of seeing churches where many of the members are committed to reaching others. It is an incredible thing to see.

Your challenge today is to pray for your church, specifically to pray for your congregation to become a Great Commission church. Today, pray that your church will *move* more than it has in a long time.

I know you will not pray with a judgmental spirit, but with a loving spirit. If your church is not moving outwardly in Great Commission obedience, it is not a healthy, functioning church. You need to pray for the church to get well by moving. If a person can take ten thousand steps a day to move toward greater health, a church can take steps in Great Commission obedience to move toward greater health.

HOW, THEN, DO WE PRAY?

Of course, you are at liberty to pray as you feel led. Today's challenge is to pray specifically that your church will become a Great Commission church. That cannot happen unless many of the members become Great Commission Christians.

The best place to start praying is for the work of the Holy Spirit in the lives of your fellow church members. We cannot have hearts to reach the people in our community in our own power and strength. As a reminder from the challenge in

Day 2, we are told in Acts 1:8 to be witnesses *after* the power of the Holy Spirit comes upon us. It can't happen in our own power; it will happen only in God's power.

Begin, then, by praying for your fellow church members to be both convicted and empowered by God. When that happens, your church will be turned upside down by the power of God.

You might even have some specific names of members for whom to pray. For some reason, God has put their names or their faces in your mind and heart. You may not be able to articulate why you are thinking about them. You don't have to understand it completely. You just need to pray for them.

It's possible there are some barriers in your church that are hindering the work of God. Sadly, many churches are not unified. Members tend to argue about petty issues. When Paul was dealing with issues in the church at Corinth, he began his first letter by appealing for unity among the church members: "I appeal to you, dear brothers and sisters, by the authority of our Lord Jesus Christ, to live in harmony with each other. Let there be no divisions in the church. Rather, be of one mind, united in thought and purpose" (1 Corinthians 1:10).

If nothing else, you could pray this verse as a prayer for your church. If your church is not unified, it is unlikely to become a Great Commission church.

It is also vitally important to pray for your pastor and staff. They are likely under spiritual attack. They might be discouraged. They might be depressed, unable to lead your church spiritually or emotionally. In fact, this issue is so important that we will devote Day 4 to it. But there is absolutely nothing wrong with praying for your pastor today as well.

TIME TO PRAY FOR THE BODY OF CHRIST

Your church is not perfect. No church is. Churches include forgiven sinners just like you and me. Now is not the time to give up on the body of Christ. Now is the time to pray for the body of Christ.

Set this book aside for just a moment and take time to pray for your church. Pray that the members of your church will become devoted Great Commission Christians. You might take five minutes to pray for your church, or you might take thirty minutes. Regardless, pray that your church will move from an inward focus to an outward focus.

Like the first church in Jerusalem, may the power of God become a reality in your church: "After this prayer, the meeting place shook, and they were all filled with the Holy Spirit. Then they preached the word of God with boldness" (Acts 4:31).

Now, it is time for you to pray for your church.

Sign and date here when you have completed the third day of the thirty-day challenge to become a Great Commission Christian.

Name: ....

Date: ....

PRAYING FOR YOUR PASTOR

Have you ever dreamed of starting a movement? Seriously, have you ever thought you could start something that would change the world?

You can. It's a simple but profound truth.

How?

Pray for your pastor.

When you pray for your pastor, your church's spiritual leader gets stronger. When the church's spiritual leader gets stronger, the church itself gets stronger. When the church gets stronger, it becomes more Great Commission focused. And a Great Commission church can begin a movement to change the world.

Do you see how it works?

Satan knows how it works. That's why he will do everything in his circumscribed power to distract and discourage your pastor. But you have the eternal power of God through prayer to strengthen your pastor. Believe me, your pastor needs prayer.

WHY PASTORS NEED PRAYER

It has been a while since I've been a pastor of a church, but I work with pastors almost every day through my organization, Church Answers. I could tell you countless stories of why pastors need prayer, but one recent conversation I had with a pastor will suffice.

Pastor "Jeremy" was being considered by a church to become their pastor. The church used a pastor search team of church members to make a recommendation to the congregation. The search team sent a list of twenty-one "expectations" to Jeremy. This one was number three on the list: "You must be accessible to the members of the church as their shepherd. You must be available 24/7/365. You are to be available to members including, but not limited to, weddings, funerals, visitations, counseling, hospital outreach, and home visitations."

Jeremy had never heard of a church that seriously expected their pastor to be on call every minute of the year. There goes the vacation! He thought it must be an overstatement, or at least a figurative statement to make a point. In response, a member of the search committee communicated to Jeremy that he would likely have to work 120 hours per week. That's an average workday of more than seventeen hours.

I gave him my counsel: "Run, Forrest, run!"

On the one hand, I was angered by the church's unreasonable expectations. On the other hand, I was grateful they were willing to make their expectations known up front. Many churches have similar expectations, in practice, but never articulate them.

At Church Answers, I have asked the same question to a few hundred pastors: What are some of your consistent and greatest distractions as a pastor? They were effusive with their responses.

"Unreasonable expectations" was near the top of the list. Though none of the pastors articulated the extreme situation that Jeremy encountered, many of the stories were similar in sentiment. One pastor was summoned to a church business meeting called to fire him because he did not return from an overseas twenty-fifth wedding anniversary trip to conduct the funeral of someone he had never met. The deceased was the deacon chairman's uncle.

I once asked twelve deacons to write down the minimum number of hours per week they expected me to devote to certain tasks and responsibilities as their pastor. They could put any items they desired, but I provided them with some options: sermon preparation, counseling, hospital visitation, community involvement, community outreach, committee and business meetings, nursing home visitation, weddings, funerals, and several others.

When I tallied the results, I was astounded. In order to meet the *minimum* expectations of just those twelve church members, I would have to work 187 hours per week. There are only 168 hours in a week.

Pastors also face constant criticism from church members. Unfortunately, many churches have become inwardly focused with church members expecting the pastor to satisfy all of their preferences and demands. And because pastors cannot possibly satisfy every preference of every church member, they often receive withering criticism.

Serving as a pastor can be excruciatingly lonely. Many times pastors are so busy taking care of others, they have little time for themselves. Many do not have meaningful friendships. And many admit to struggling to care for their own families.

Most pastors struggle financially because they are woefully underpaid. An elder of a church once told me that they underpaid their pastor intentionally. They believed that if he struggled financially, he would have greater humility and be more dependent on God. I doubt that elder was working on his own sanctification in the same manner.

I could continue, but you get the point. Our pastors need

our prayers. It is difficult to have a healthy church if the pastor is not healthy spiritually. It is difficult to have a Great Commission church if the pastor is dealing with emotionally draining demands and expectations.

Thus, the challenge for Day 4 is to pray for your pastor. You might already know how you plan to pray. If not, here are a few suggestions to guide you.

HOW DO I PRAY FOR MY PASTOR?

Above all, pray that your pastor will have a close walk with God. This means we should be praying for the prayer life of our pastors. We should pray that the Holy Spirit will both guide and comfort them. Pray that your pastor will regularly hear from God through prayer and Scripture reading.

Always pray for the pastor's family. Healthy relationships with his spouse and children are vital if your pastor is to lead well. Paul's words to his protégé Timothy were unambiguous: "If a man cannot manage his own household, how can he take care of God's church?" (1 Timothy 3:5).

When I ask pastors how I can pray for them, they often tell me to pray for their preaching. That includes not only the actual delivery of the sermon, but also the hours of preparation that go into sermon study and writing. It would be good if you include this matter in your prayers for your pastor.

More pastors are expressing vulnerability and transparency

when they ask for prayer for their emotional lives. Over the past several years, more pastors have shared with me about their ongoing struggles with depression. Sadly, pastor suicides seem to be on the rise. While I don't have the data that can confirm the pastoral suicide rate, at the very least, this issue has become prominent with many well-known pastors taking their lives.

Also, pray for your pastor as a leader. For sure, pastors are first servants, but they must also serve as servant leaders on a regular basis. Your church is an organization they must lead. They are often expected to lead meetings. In your church you might have part-time or full-time staff the pastor is expected to lead. And you certainly want your pastor to lead your church to become a Great Commission church.

These are some of the areas you can pray for your pastor. You likely have some other ideas how to pray.

PRAYING FOR MY PASTOR

I finished writing this chapter on a Saturday night. Often, I will pause on Saturday evenings to pray for my pastor for his preaching the next day. As I have written these words, I am reminded again of two realities.

First, serving as a pastor is difficult. Indeed, outside of God's call and strength, it is impossible. Second, praying for my pastor's preaching is good, but there are many other areas where I can and should pray for him. Tonight, I will take a bit of extra time to pray for my pastor.

I thank God for my pastor.

Now, it is time for you to respond to the Day 4 challenge and pray for your pastor.

Sign and date here when you have completed the fourth day of the thirty-day challenge to become a Great Commission Christian.

Name: ....

Date: ....

PRAYING FOR GREAT COMMISSION CHURCH MEMBERS

It's inspiring to watch a great team working together. Though you might assume I'm referring to sports teams, my thoughts are not limited to athletics. Business teams. Community teams. Mission teams. Medical teams. There are many possibilities.

Two prominent characteristics of great teams I have seen are *unity* and *chemistry*. Obviously, the two are related. Competency and talent are also important, of course. Most good teams will exhibit those traits. But most of the *great* teams I've seen have great chemistry and work in unity. Some teams with less talent have defeated more gifted teams by working in greater harmony.

Chemistry and unity are of particular importance in the

church. The healthiest churches I have seen have members who put the entire body before themselves. They put the good of the gospel before their own preferences.

On this fifth day, the challenge is to pray for your fellow church members, particularly that they would have hearts and passion for the Great Commission. Here are some specific ideas for prayer.

UNITY

As noted above, unity is important for a church to have a Great Commission focus. If you doubt the importance of unity among Christians, remember these words of Jesus: "I pray that they will all be one, just as you and I are one—as you are in me, Father, and I am in you. And may they be in us so that the world will believe you sent me" (John 17:21).

Don't miss Jesus' conclusion. If Christians are unified, then the world will believe the gospel. That's why this day of prayer is so important. That's why this matter of unity is one key reason we should be praying for our fellow church members.

By the way, before we proceed further, let me remind you to include yourself in your prayers for church members. We're not simply praying for "those other people." We need the same prayerful admonitions ourselves.

LOVE OF COMMUNITY

Pray that the members of your church will love the members of your community—their Jerusalem in the example of Acts 1:8. Many church members likely do not know the people in their own neighborhoods, much less the members in the community at large. Wouldn't it be great if, for example, community leaders knew your church because of the love and support they received from church members? I am familiar with a church with an average worship attendance of fifty-five that sent one thousand notes of encouragement to different community leaders in one year.

These church members told countless stories about how a number of community leaders responded with sincere appreciation. Many of them were accustomed to regular notes and emails of criticism. The positive notes stood out and became a blessing to them.

Pray for your church members to love your community.

LOVE FOR YOUR PASTOR AND STAFF

On Day 4, we guided you to pray for your pastor. Let's expand that prayer reach a bit. As part of your time praying for your church members, pray that they will love your pastor and staff more than ever. We pointed out earlier that pastors go through many trials and have many challenges. So do other staff members. They all need prayer.

They all need as many church members as possible praying for them.

Pray for your church members to love your pastor and staff. It is critical to your church becoming a Great Commission congregation.

A FOCUS ON OTHERS

Many church members today are focused on what the church can do for them. They want their kind of music. They want the sermon to be a certain length (usually shorter). They want services to be on their schedule. They want the facilities to look a certain way or be a certain color. The list of wants is endless.

When the preferences of the church members become greater than their passion for the gospel, the church is dying.

Your prayer for your fellow church members should include prayers for them to become others-focused. Putting Christ before themselves. Putting other members before themselves. Surrendering their own preferences, wants, and desires for the greater good of the church.

I have never seen a divided church that is a Great Commission church. A divided church has members who are more concerned about getting their own way than following Christ's way. Of course, Christ's way is to share the gospel with others.

Pray that the members of your church will develop an outward focus that looks toward others. And don't forget to pray for yourself as one of the members of the church.

THE MIGHTY FEW

Several years ago, I spoke with a pastor whose small church had experienced significant growth over a three-year period. The church had grown from an average attendance of forty to more than one hundred. The pastor, in all humility, said it had nothing to do with his leadership. Though I understood why he said what he did, I wasn't sure I could fully agree.

Three years earlier, an elder in the church had fallen under conviction that his gospel witness was anemic. In fact, he couldn't remember the last time he had told someone how Christ had changed his life. And he could not remember when he had last invited someone to church.

He told another elder about this conviction, and the two men agreed that they would pray for gospel opportunities and would hold each other accountable. Within about two months, seven other people had joined this informal accountability group. Most of the new additions were women, so the group comprised three men and six women.

There was no formal program, no major announcement was made to the church, and no system for gauging progress was established. The nine church members simply prayed for Great Commission opportunities, and they shared with the others in the group, primarily by email, how God was moving them toward a Great Commission focus.

About five months into this new endeavor, two new people joined the church. Both were new Christians and were somehow connected to one of the nine praying church members. Over the next three years, the steady flow of new Christians into the church continued unabated. There never was a massive influx, just a remarkably steady addition of people whose lives had been affected by the gospel.

"We didn't even realize that our church had more than doubled in size in those three years," one of the two elders said. "We just made a commitment and stuck with it. It's amazing what God will do when his people are obedient and committed."

GREAT COMMISSION MEMBERS

The elder's statement is both simple and profound: "We just made a commitment and stuck with it." The results were equally simple and profound: "It's amazing what God will do when his people are obedient and committed."

As you have no doubt realized by now, we are emphasizing the power of prayer in these early days of the thirty-day challenge. A church will never become a Great Commission church in its own strength. It takes the power of God. And prayer is not simply a prelude; it is the essential catalyst of a Great Commission church.

Take a few minutes now to pray for the members of your church. You can use some of the suggestions we noted, but don't feel constrained by any specific list. As the apostle James noted, "The earnest prayer of a righteous person has great power and produces wonderful results" (James 5:16).

As you continue to pray throughout the thirty days, your prayers will produce wonderful results, including seeing others in your church become Great Commission Christians.

Sign and date here when you have completed the fifth day of the thirty-day challenge to become a Great Commission Christian.

Name: ....

Date: ....

PRAYING FOR THE POWER OF THE HOLY SPIRIT

If something needs to be fixed at our house, my wife calls a repairman.

Let me repeat that with greater transparency. If *anything* needs to be fixed at our house, my wife calls a repairman.

Yes, that is because I am totally inept at any kind of repair work. It's not just that I can't fix things; I tend to make the problem worse.

As an example of my ineptitude, I have, on several occasions, declared that something was irreversibly broken, only to discover that it wasn't plugged in. I can see my wife rolling her eyes even as I write these words. Her observations are typically right to the point: "It's hard for the thing to work if it has no power."

I'm sure you can see where I'm going with this. It's hard for the church to accomplish its mission if it isn't plugged in to the power source. Jesus himself said we must have the power of the Holy Spirit for the church to function as he intends (Luke 24:49; John 14:26; Acts 1:8; 4:31).

WAIT ON THE SPIRIT

Certain passages in the book of Acts are considered paradigmatic moments in the early history of the church. For example, Acts 1:8 is one of the more well-known Great Commission passages. Acts 2:1-4 describes the coming and indwelling of the Holy Spirit to believers in Christ. Acts 9 tells the story of the conversion of Saul (later called Paul) on the road to Damascus.

Another important passage in Acts precedes those noted above. The scene takes place in Acts 1:4-5, where Jesus is eating with his disciples. Jesus says, "Do not leave Jerusalem until the Father sends you the gift he promised, as I told you before. John baptized with water, but in just a few days you will be baptized with the Holy Spirit."

The early followers of Christ were to be indwelt by the Holy Spirit and empowered by the Holy Spirit. Again, Jesus spoke of the coming power of the Spirit when he told his followers right before his ascension, "You will receive power when the Holy Spirit comes upon you" (Acts 1:8).

The commands are clear. Wait. Wait on the Holy Spirit. Wait for his power.

HIS COMMAND AND OUR RESPONSE

As we have been preparing for Great Commission power by praying and looking at key passages of Scripture, in a sense we have been waiting. We have been waiting to be fully prayed up and fully empowered.

Paul writes this command in Ephesians 5:18-19: "Don't be drunk with wine, because that will ruin your life. Instead, be filled with the Holy Spirit, singing psalms and hymns and spiritual songs among yourselves, and making music to the Lord in your hearts." Because the wording is in the imperative in the original language, we know that to be filled with the Spirit is a command.

We will take this sixth day of the challenge to pray that we will be filled with and empowered by the Holy Spirit. The Great Commission is not a spiritual sales pitch designed for someone to buy. It is an offer from God to receive forgiveness of sins and the promise of eternity. It cannot be regarded lightly. It cannot be accomplished in our own power.

We must pray for the power of the Holy Spirit as we seek to be Great Commission Christians. We cannot go forward without it.

PRAYING FOR THE FRUIT OF THE SPIRIT

Her name was Stephanie Jackson. She died as a young lady in her thirties, leaving behind her husband and a preschool boy she adored. The cancer was swift and unrelenting.

We met Stephanie through Church Answers. By "we," I mean a few thousand pastors and church leaders who got to know Stephanie and love her through our key communication hub called Church Answers Central.

I have rarely known someone who exhibited the fruit of the Spirit like Stephanie did. She was always encouraging. Always smiling. Always helpful. Always kind. When someone challenged her, she would exclaim, "That's a great point!"

I miss her. Many of us miss her.

What is the fruit of the Spirit? It is when "the Holy Spirit produces this kind of fruit in our lives: love, joy, peace, patience, kindness, goodness, faithfulness, gentleness, and self-control" (Galatians 5:22-23).

As we pause on Day 6 to pray for the power of the Holy Spirit, we are concurrently praying that the fruit of the Spirit would continually be evident in our lives. When we have the power of the Holy Spirit in our lives, we supernaturally manifest the fruit of the Spirit.

Pray, then, for the power of the Holy Spirit. Pray as well for the fruit of the Spirit.

By the way, we named our highest annual award at Church Answers the Stephanie Jackson Award. Stephanie is in heaven, but the fruit of her work lives on.

PRAYING FOR THE GOSPEL AND THE GREAT COMMISSION

Why are we devoting a day in our thirty-day challenge to pray for the power of the Holy Spirit? So we can become Great Commission Christians and our churches can become Great Commission congregations.

When you have the power of the Holy Spirit in your life, he will open your eyes to opportunities every day. If you are serious about yielding control of your life to the Holy Spirit, you will be amazed at the people and situations that come your way.

Remember what Jesus said about opportunities? "The harvest is great, but the workers are few. So pray to the Lord who is in charge of the harvest; ask him to send more workers into his fields" (Matthew 9:37-38). The opportunities are great. The harvest is great. When we have the power of the Spirit, we see those opportunities.

When we have the power of the Spirit, we have the ability to know what to say, when to say it, and when to listen. For years, I worried about how I would respond to certain situations and questions when I shared the gospel or simply invited someone to church. But those imagined scenarios never happened. God always gave me the right response. It has taken me years to grasp it, but I really don't have to worry about whether I will say something precisely right, because God will give me the words.

Has there ever been a time when you thought you did a terrible job of sharing the gospel with someone, but it didn't seem to matter? I remember being nervous and stumbling over my words while inviting someone to church, yet the Spirit was at work nonetheless. The man I invited came to church the next Sunday and eventually became a follower of Christ. When we have the power of the Spirit, we don't have to rely on our own eloquence.

When you pray for the power of the Holy Spirit, you are welcoming him to control your life. You are asking him to give you the thoughts, words, and actions to be a Great Commission Christian. And though all the prayers you will be praying during these thirty days are important, this one might be the most important. You are praying to yield your life to the Holy Spirit so that you can become a Great Commission Christian.

Take a few minutes and pray for the power of the Holy Spirit in your life. Pray that the Spirit will mold you into a powerful witness for Christ. He will indeed shape you to become a Great Commission Christian.

Sign and date here when you have completed the sixth day of the thirty-day challenge to become a Great Commission Christian.

Name: ....

Date: ....

THAT THING CALLED COURAGE

What is the most courageous thing you've done? I have read many stories of courage, but one comes immediately to mind.

On March 7, 2022, the massive Sunshine Skyway Bridge over Tampa Bay, Florida, was closed as part of a 10K race for the armed forces. Nearly seven thousand runners were on the bridge. Suddenly, a drunk driver broke through all the barricades and headed at a high rate of speed toward the runners.

Florida Highway Patrol trooper Toni Schuck, sitting in her patrol car near the bridge, saw the approaching disaster. Realizing that her vehicle was the only thing standing between the out-of-control driver and thousands of defenseless runners, Trooper Schuck put her vehicle in drive and headed straight toward the speeding car.

When the two vehicles met, nearly head-on, the sound of crashing metal echoed across the bay.

Miraculously, both Trooper Schuck and the drunk driver survived. They were seriously injured, but they survived. Later, Trooper Schuck told her story.

"I was the last officer—I knew that. I knew it was me. So, if it wasn't me to get her to stop, then who? I don't know."[2]

We hear about stories of courage every week. We laud those who have taken such heroic steps, particularly when they put their lives on the line. We wonder whether we would do the same if confronted with a similar situation.

COURAGE TO SPEAK ABOUT JESUS

This next story about courage comes directly from the Bible. Pause for a moment to read Acts 4:1-31. When you're done, let's unpack it a bit.

You really need the context of Acts 3 to fully understand Acts 4. A beggar who was a mainstay feature next to a gate at the Temple in Jerusalem had been lame since birth. For years, friends or relatives had carried him to the same spot each day to beg. But when he encountered the apostles Peter and John one day, he was healed by the power of Jesus. In an instant, this man who had been disabled his entire life was jumping for joy and praising God.

Though many people in Jerusalem were astounded and joyful about the healing, some key leaders, particularly religious leaders were concerned and upset. They feared that this healing in Jesus' name would give major credibility to the gospel, which they opposed. They were concerned that the name of Jesus was becoming too pervasive and powerful. It threatened their leadership and their authority.

Acts 4 opens with a confrontation between the two apostles and "the priests, the captain of the Temple guard, and some of the Sadducees" (Acts 4:1). When Peter and John were subsequently arrested and cast into prison, they knew what awaited them. They would be confronted with a choice. Either stop talking about Jesus or face imprisonment or even death.

Here's what I love about Acts 4. Nowhere does it suggest that Peter and John debated about what they should do. They knew they only had one choice, the path of obedience to speak about Jesus.

Do you wonder what you would do in a similar situation? Do you wonder whether you would have the courage to continue to speak about Jesus, even if it meant death or imprisonment? Do you wonder whether you would have courage?

POWER AND COURAGE

As they likely expected, Peter and John were told to stop speaking about Jesus. Look at Acts 4:16-18:

> "What should we do with these men?" they asked each other. "We can't deny that they have performed a miraculous sign, and everybody in Jerusalem knows about it. But to keep them from spreading their propaganda any further, we must warn them not to speak to anyone in Jesus' name again." So they called the apostles back in and commanded them never again to speak or teach in the name of Jesus."

There you have it. The order from the authorities was clear: Stop talking about Jesus. The consequences of disobedience were equally clear. After all, they were already in prison. But Peter and John never considered acquiescing. After all, they had been an instrument of the power of God to see a hopelessly lame man healed and jumping for joy. God's power would be with them now as well.

Their response was to the point: "Do you think God wants us to obey you rather than him? We cannot stop telling about everything we have seen and heard" (Acts 4:19-20).

Their obedience to God was rewarded. Their trust in him and his power resulted in their being released:

> The council then threatened them further, but they finally let them go because they didn't know how to punish them without starting a riot. For everyone was praising God for this miraculous sign—the healing of a man who had been lame for more than forty years.
>
> ACTS 4:21-22

A PRAYER FOR YOUR COURAGE

It is unlikely you will face imprisonment or death for talking to someone about Jesus or inviting someone to church. In fact, it is unlikely you will get a harsh rejection. You might get excuses. You might get a bit of a debate. You might even experience some level of social ostracism. But you probably won't go to jail or be put to death.

Still, it takes courage to talk about Jesus. It takes courage to invite someone to church. And you will always hear those words of discouragement in your mind. You can always find excuses to say, "Not now." You will always have distractions to get your mind off those things that Jesus desires.

So, don't be shy or ashamed to pray for courage. Don't think you are weak or unusual for asking for God's strength.

To the contrary, your desire to pray for courage is a clear sign you are living in God's strength.

WHEN COURAGE GOES TO CHURCH

After Peter and John were released, they returned to the other believers who were gathered. This incipient church could not wait to get the report from the two men. Their reaction? "When they heard the report, all the believers lifted their voices together in prayer" (Acts 4:24).

The entire church was encouraged by this great act of God. They were moved to prayer. Indeed, the edification and power were so strong that they had a physical and spiritual effect on the gathered believers: "After this prayer, the meeting place shook, and they were all filled with the Holy Spirit. Then they preached the word of God with boldness" (Acts 4:31).

So, our primary task today is to read and understand this portion of Acts 4. The passage is a powerful and poignant reminder of the work of God through our obedience. It is also a reminder that courage does not come to us naturally, but it is given to us supernaturally.

Take time to read Acts 4 again closely. Use it to guide your prayer life as you pray for yourself and others in your church to be men and women of courage.

By the way, congratulations for completing the first week

of the thirty-day challenge. We will have a few more days of prayer; then we will be ready to move forward in gospel obedience. God is already at work in your life and in your church.

Sign and date here when you have completed the seventh day of the thirty-day challenge to become a Great Commission Christian.

Name: ....

Date: ....

TO LOVE MY COMMUNITY

I am an introvert. Though my personality can't be an excuse for failing to love and connect with people, I do have my challenges. It took a pandemic for me to move beyond my introversion to connect with people in my neighborhood.

Though it may seem unlikely I would overcome my worst introversion tendencies during a pandemic, it really did happen. When the quarantine first took effect, most of us in the neighborhood became restless after sitting at home for days. And like many of my neighbors, I decided to take walks almost every day.

Looking back, it seems surreal. Our streets don't typically have many walkers, but they were flooded with people desiring to see something other than their interior walls. I also remember how we kept our masks on and maintained six feet of separation between us.

Despite the social distancing and the masks, my neighbors and I talked each day as we walked the same streets. I got to know my neighbors better. And like most situations when we see other people face-to-face, even with our faces covered, we learn to appreciate each other more.

I had numerous opportunities to speak about my faith during those walks. The conversations were never forced or awkward. My neighbors and I felt comfortable talking about the things that mattered to us as we grew more appreciative of each other.

I realized I was learning to love my neighbors.

LOVING YOUR NEIGHBOR TO LOVE YOUR COMMUNITY

An expert in religious law asked Jesus the most important question:

> "Teacher, what should I do to inherit eternal life?"
> Jesus replied, "What does the law of Moses say?
> How do you read it?" The man answered, "'You
> must love the LORD your God with all your heart,
> all your soul, all your strength, and all your mind.'
> And, 'Love your neighbor as yourself.'"
>
> LUKE 10:25-27

But the man wanted deeper details, so he challenged Jesus: "And who is my neighbor?" (Luke 10:29). That was the question that led Jesus to tell the parable of the Good Samaritan. In the famous story, Jesus reminds us that the word *neighbor* is broad and inclusive. It particularly applies to people we may regard as unlikeable or even as enemies.

As a consequence of this parable, an entire genre has developed, expounding on the concept of being a good neighbor. And as the parable points out, "our neighbor" includes *everyone* who lives in close proximity to us, whether we feel a sense of affinity with them or not. This includes people on both sides of the tracks—from the tree-lined streets to the apartment complexes, and those living along the roads in rural communities.

On Day 8 of this thirty-day challenge, we are praying for our communities. Start by praying for those who live in closest proximity to you and expand your vision as the Holy Spirit leads you.

To become Great Commission Christians, we must reach our Jerusalem. We must reach our communities. And we begin by praying for our neighbors.

If you're like me, you may barely know some of the people on your street or in your neighborhood. Now is the time to pray for opportunities to meet them and talk with them. It took a pandemic for me to get to know my neighbors better, but you can find more subtle ways to connect with them.

Your community begins with your neighbors. Pray for them.

PRAY FOR YOUR DEMOGRAPHIC COMMUNITY

Your demographic community is the place of your home address. For my wife and me, it is Franklin, Tennessee. Your church is located in a demographic community. Your church's address is no accident. God put your church where it is to be a gospel presence in that community.

I realized not too long ago that I didn't often pray specifically for Franklin. That omission has been rectified. I now pray for my community regularly. If you are praying for the people in a specific place, it is likely you will learn to love the place and the people more. And if you love them more, the love of Christ will be evident in your interactions in your community.

During the pandemic, I closed my offices and started working from home. Most of the employees of my company, Church Answers, are scattered throughout the United States (and a couple in other countries), so I did not think I needed an office beyond my own home.

For a number of reasons, however, I made the decision to return to an office. One of those reasons was my desire to connect with other workers in Franklin. Now my office is right downtown on Main Street. I am getting to know people better every day. That move has also helped me love and pray for my community more.

PRAY FOR THE LEADERS AND MERCHANTS IN YOUR COMMUNITY

On Day 11, you will be encouraged to write a note to someone in your community. It could be as simple as a word of encouragement. It might also be a note that lets them know you've prayed for them.

Today, I'm asking you to pray for one or more people specifically in your community. Consider praying for some of the leaders. Leaders in most communities face challenges every day. They face critics. You may need to look up a city directory online to see who your political leaders are. Or you can look up the law enforcement officials or other first responders. These are all opportunities to pray for your community leaders.

If you have access to a local community publication, look for stories about people in your community. Almost every day, I come across a story about a key leader or person in Franklin. It's a reminder to me that I need to be praying for those people.

As a typical introvert, I become more comfortable with people as I see them more often and get to know them better. I make a point to get my hair cut by the same person and to use the same handyman regularly. My handyman is now a good friend because my wife has asked me often enough to call him before I mess something up.

I even use a grocery delivery service (a classic introvert's choice) where I can choose the same shopper every time.

I have come to know and even love these friends and merchants in the community. I am thus reminded to pray for them more consistently.

PRAY FOR POINTS OF PAIN AND PEOPLE IN PAIN

Every community has some type of deep and identifiable need. For some it is drug addiction and the common corollary of homelessness. For some it is teen suicide. For some it is major unemployment. For some it is the breakdown of relationships in our homes and schools.

Every community has a deep need, and every deep need has faces and people connected to it. As you pray for your community, take time to discover those needs. Something as simple as reading a local publication will probably suffice. Pray for the needs you see, and for the people affected by those needs.

On Day 8 we are seeking to love our communities more deeply and more personally. As we love our communities, we are compelled to pray for them more. And as we pray for them more, we learn to love them more.

Pause for a few moments and show love for your community by praying for it. Use the suggestions on these pages or add your own. You certainly know your community better than I do. Take time to pray for your home community right now.

Sign and date here when you have completed the eighth day of the thirty-day challenge to become a Great Commission Christian.

Name: ....

Date: ....

TO OBEY IS BETTER THAN SACRIFICE

I remember well my first conversations with Frank. He was a coworker at the bank where I worked when I was in seminary.

Frank knew that I had been a successful bank executive before I answered the call to vocational ministry. He knew I had returned to banking part-time just to put food on the table. He knew, or could have surmised, that my pay had gone from an executive salary to that of an hourly employee.

But Frank did not understand this.

How could I give up the fast-paced life and good income to end up selling all my possessions and working for a relatively paltry pay? What kind of person does that?

Frank asked a ton of questions. When I attempted to explain what Christ had done in my life, he countered defensively with his own good deeds. "Hey, I'm a good person," he said, with certainty that his overall character was equal to or better than mine. Or he would point out how he helped someone with a business plan that was "making a boatload of money every year."

Frank was convinced that his sacrificial behavior was sufficient for God. It seemed like he kept an internal scorecard where he felt like his good deeds were more than his bad deeds. My efforts to explain grace to him seemed to fall on deaf ears. He just stared at me when I explained Romans 3:23: "For everyone has sinned; we all fall short of God's glorious standard."

The prophet Samuel had a challenge with King Saul. The king wanted to demonstrate all the sacrifices he had made on God's behalf. He wanted to convince the prophet that his good outweighed his bad. Samuel spoke forcefully and bravely to the king: "What is more pleasing to the LORD: your burnt offerings and sacrifices or your obedience to his voice? Listen! Obedience is better than sacrifice" (1 Samuel 15:22).

For Day 9, we will focus on praying for our own obedience. We will pray that we clearly hear God's commands and admonitions. And we will pray that we will be obedient to them. We will seek to know with greater clarity that obedience is better than sacrifice.

When I left that bank to become a pastor, I felt sorrow

and even a bit of guilt that I had been unable to communicate the truths of the gospel to Frank. Though I knew I shouldn't carry the burden, I admit that I felt like a failure.

But God continued to work in Frank's life. I didn't hear from Frank for thirty years—until he called me one day at my office. Thirty years down the road he wanted to talk to me!

We were both living in Nashville, and he asked if he could come see me at my home. I welcomed him gladly. The man who came into my house was a different man than I had known three decades earlier. He no longer had the bold self-assurance I remembered. And he looked sick, very sick.

Frank told me he was dying. The doctors had told him he had about six more months, and that proved to be accurate. During those six months, Frank and I talked many times. I visited his home. We talked about faith. We talked about the step of obedience of becoming a follower of Christ. Frank repented of his sins. By faith, he accepted the grace of our Lord Jesus Christ.

Frank became a Christian.

In his final days, he asked me to officiate his funeral. I was able to tell his friends from different walks of life that Frank was in heaven. I was able to tell them how they could go to heaven.

Never underestimate the power of God to change someone's life.

Obedience to him leads to eternal life.

THAT FIRST STEP OF OBEDIENCE

The call of Christ is an invitation to obediently follow him, to embrace him as Lord and Savior. It is an acknowledgment of our sins. Again, Romans 3:23 says it well: "Everyone has sinned; we all fall short of God's glorious standard." No one measures up on their own merit. Everyone has sinned, and that sin separates us from God's holy perfection. There is no way that we ourselves can bridge that gap.

Our obedience begins when we not only acknowledge our sin, but also desire to turn away from our sin. It is what the Bible calls *repentance*. The apostle Paul spoke cogently about repentance: "I never shrank back from telling you what you needed to hear, either publicly or in your homes. I have had one message for Jews and Greeks alike—the necessity of repenting from sin and turning to God, and of having faith in our Lord Jesus" (Acts 20:20-21).

Paul often spoke of repentance and faith in the same breath, much like he does in Acts 20:21. Repentance is the act of "turning from." Faith is the act of "turning to." When we move away from something, we are simultaneously moving toward something else. We move away from sin (repentance) and move toward Christ (faith).

The Christian's first step of obedience is when we repent from sin and place our faith in Jesus Christ. When we do, we are given a new life. We are born again. We had a physical birth. Now we have a spiritual birth. We have been obedient and have chosen to follow Christ as Lord and Savior.

OBEDIENCE TO A COMMISSION

It is clear that Jesus has a command he wants Christians to obey. Though there are different places in Scripture where we can find the command, we looked at Acts 1:8 in detail on Day 2: "You will receive power when the Holy Spirit comes upon you. And you will be my witnesses, telling people about me everywhere—in Jerusalem, throughout Judea, in Samaria, and to the ends of the earth."

We call this command, and others like it (such as Matthew 28:19-20), the Great Commission. The terminology is not incidental. It is indeed one of the greatest commands we have to obey. If we have become followers of Christ, we are commanded to tell others about Jesus and what he has done in our lives.

The action step for Day 9 of the thirty-day challenge is another prayer: "Lord, help me to be obedient to your Great Commission. Give me your power, strength, and discernment in my life as I share with others what Jesus has done for me."

Don't allow the simplicity of the prayer to diminish its importance. You're praying that God will give you everything you need to obey the Great Commission.

Note that you are not praying for a certain methodology; you are simply praying for obedience. That obedience may come in the form of inviting someone to church where they can hear the gospel and become positively influenced by other believers. The obedience may come by simply praying to God each day for an opportunity to share the love of Christ in word or in deed. The obedience may happen when someone like Frank comes into your life and asks you point-blank questions.

Like the other days we have dedicated to prayer, Day 9 is an important day. When we ask God to help us become more obedient, he is pleased to respond positively. On this particular day, we are praying for obedience to the Great Commission. We are praying not only for opportunities, but also that we will do exactly what God wants us to do when those opportunities arise.

Take a moment now and pray for obedience, particularly obedience to the Great Commission.

Sign and date here when you have completed the ninth day of the thirty-day challenge to become a Great Commission Christian.

Name: ....

Date: ....

PRAYING FOR YOUR ONE

"Your one" refers to someone you know, perhaps someone with whom you have frequent contact. Your one should be someone who is not a Christian or perhaps someone who is not connected with a local church fellowship. The idea behind praying for your one is to ask God for the Holy Spirit to draw this person to salvation or to connect him or her with a church.

Several years ago, I began focusing for the first time on praying for my one. His name was Roy, and he cut my hair on a regular basis. Roy was a bit old-fashioned. On occasion, when I would introduce Roy to someone as my "stylist," he would correct me. "I don't know what a stylist is, but I'm not one," he said. "I'm a barber."

You can start to get to know someone after several haircuts with the same barber. Here is what Roy told me. He had been divorced twice, and he wasn't going to get married a third time. He told me he was either bad at choosing wives or not that great as a husband. I think he concluded that the answer was some of both.

Roy had had polio as a child. As a consequence, he wore a metal brace on his leg. Other than telling me why he had the brace, he never mentioned his leg again. He never complained about it either.

But the joy of Roy's life was his daughter. If I remember correctly, she was born when Roy was in his fifties. Roy considered his daughter his "old age gift in life."

I told Roy several times what Jesus had done in my life. I invited him to church almost every time I got a haircut.

On one occasion, Roy told me about his fears of being a single dad. He wanted what was best for his daughter, but he wasn't sure what that was. I responded to him with no forethought, "You better get her in church." That did it. You could see the light go on.

Roy and his daughter showed up at my church the next Sunday. They eventually became active in a church closer to their home. And they became followers of Christ.

Roy was my one. Including Roy's daughter, God gave me two.

I moved out of the city where I met Roy, but I always went

to him to get my hair cut whenever I was in town. Years later, I got a call that Roy had died of cancer. He had requested of his family that I do the funeral. I was honored. It was my joy.

THE GREAT INTERSECTION

Praying for your one provides a great intersection between evangelism and prayer. You are depending on the power of prayer and the work of the Holy Spirit to change the person's heart as you pray and continue to share your faith. Let me share with you several lessons I've learned from people who have discovered this intersection by praying for their one.

Many people have told us at Church Answers that God opens their eyes when they pray for their one. They not only see the one with clearer spiritual vision, but their eyes are also opened to more opportunities for prayer and ministry. Praying for your one typically leads to opportunities for more than one.

We've also heard that praying for your one makes conversations about spiritual matters so much easier. Martha, a church member in Wichita, told us, "I used to cringe at having spiritual conversations with people who aren't Christians. Now, it seems like God opens natural paths for relating to people. I don't have the nervousness I once had."

Many people who have prayed for their one report that they have become more involved in their churches. When they see the needs of people outside the church, they have a desire to serve more eagerly inside their church.

Praying for your one is the intersection of prayer and evangelism. It is on behalf of the one who is the focus of the prayers. And it is for the one who prays.

PREPARING FOR DAY 11

On Day 10 of this thirty-day challenge, you will pray for one person specifically. But when you turn the page tomorrow, you will be challenged to also write a note to someone. The person you write to could be the same person you're praying for today, but it doesn't have to be. But you will inevitably be drawn to connect with your one in different ways. The more you pray for someone, the more your heart will be prepared to serve them.

So start thinking ahead. As you pray for your one, what are some other ways to connect with him or her? Is the best connection an email? Is it an invitation to coffee or a meal? Is it a small gift of appreciation? The possibilities are endless. As you pray, you will find a number of ways to serve and connect with your one.

MORE THAN ONE PERSON, MORE THAN ONE DAY

These thirty days of challenges are guidelines, not restrictions. Indeed, I hope you will pray for your one on more than Day 10. In fact, don't be surprised if you are reminded on other days of this possibility. A brief daily prayer is neither a burden nor something that takes a lot of time. In fact, you can pray for God to bring your one to your mind and heart on a regular basis.

Praying for your one also doesn't mean that you must limit your prayer to only one person. When I made Roy my one, his daughter became an obvious person who should also be a part of my prayer life. I started praying for one, but I took joy in praying for two.

Okay, have you decided who your one will be? Is it someone with whom you work? Is it a merchant you see regularly, someone like Roy? Is it someone in your school, perhaps in your own class? Is it someone from your past, and you simply feel led to pray for that person? Pause here until you have a name firmly in mind.

DECIDE AND PRAY (AND PRAY AGAIN)

We met Nona in a consultation our team was doing at her church. Many of the church members mentioned Nona when we interviewed them as part of the consultation. We found out that she had been praying for her one for more than nine years.

When I interviewed Nona, I was intrigued by her influence in this church and among the members. She smiled with modesty and told me it was really very simple. She just started praying for a specific person, and her plans were to continue to pray for that person daily until one of three things happened: the person became a Christian, became active in a church, or died.

Actually, over the past nine years, Nona had prayed for twenty-six ones. Of those, twenty-four had become Christians or had become active in a church. One had died. And one was still "in progress," to use Nona's words.

Sometimes it takes more than a year of praying for your one before you see results. Sometimes it takes only a few weeks.

Your challenge today is to select and begin praying for your one. His or her life will be changed.

And so will yours.

Sign and date here when you have completed the tenth day of the thirty-day challenge to become a Great Commission Christian.

Name: ....

Date: ....

DAY 11

WRITING OUTWARDLY

Today's action step might require expanding the boundaries of your comfort zone. For the first ten days of this challenge, you have primarily been praying for people or looking at Scripture. Today, I will ask you to write a note to someone.

I anticipate that you may have some questions at this point. To whom do I write? What do I say? What if I hardly know the person? Isn't writing to someone out of the blue a bit weird?

I get it. It can indeed be uncomfortable. Let's answer some important questions before you get started.

DOES THIS COMMUNICATION HAVE TO BE HANDWRITTEN?

When was the last time you wrote a letter by hand? I bet it's been three or four years for me. My son Sam is a master letter writer. He writes a few letters each week by hand, addresses the envelopes by hand, and puts a stamp on them to mail. I wish I had his discipline.

Does the letter have to be written by hand? Not necessarily. But if you are able and willing to do so, your letter will have a much greater impact. Think about the last time you received a real handwritten letter or note. Do you remember how special you felt that someone had taken the time to write to you? Do you remember how grateful you were to that person?

So, yes, handwritten letters are better, but they aren't mandatory for this exercise.

If you have the person's phone number, you can send him or her a text. A text message has a greater sense of personalization than an email, though not as much as a handwritten note. I have a few friends who text me encouraging messages on occasion. I am always grateful and motivated to do the same for them and others.

Of course, you can email the person, if that's the best way to make contact. But emails carry risks. They can be overlooked with the barrage of emails people receive every day. They can go to a spam folder. They are often not read on a regular basis. Still, an email is better than no communication. The most important factor is that you write to someone.

TO WHOM DO I WRITE?

The ideal person to write to is your *one* from Day 10. If you have an established relationship and the person's address, email, or phone number, you can write to him or her immediately. If your one is someone you hardly know, it might be premature to write to them.

One of my favorite "one" stories is about my garbage pickup service. I live just outside the city limits of Franklin, Tennessee, so we have to contract with a private service. When I moved to Franklin, several people recommended a family-owned business. I immediately discovered why they had recommended this company.

Quite frankly, I didn't think I would ever be impressed by a garbage pickup service, but I was by these folks. They told me to leave the trash at the back of my house and they would pick it up there. They didn't want me to have to leave a trash can in the front of the house. "It just doesn't look good," the co-owner told me. Moreover, they never leave even the smallest piece of trash behind. I watched one day after the wind had blown some debris around. Two men got out of the truck and picked up every piece.

The workers are friendly as well. They always greet me

if I'm outside. They often wave to me as I pass them in the neighborhood.

One day, I decided to write the owners a handwritten letter of thanks. Yes, it was a first for me to write a garbage pickup service. I also included a small monetary gift of thanks. Their gratitude to me was unbelievable. One of the workers became my one, and we've had a number of gospel conversations.

You can write to a merchant like I did. It took me but a minute to find their address online. When you write to a merchant, it's always better if it's someone you will see on a regular basis. I currently have four ones, and they are all local merchants. I have written to three of the four.

You may decide to write to a family member or relative. Or you may have an opportunity to send a text to a friend or neighbor.

For this particular exercise, it is important to write to someone who is not a Christian—or, at the very least, is not active in a church. Though you can certainly write encouraging notes to anyone, the act of writing to someone who is not a follower of Christ is a major step in becoming a Great Commission Christian.

WHAT DO I SAY?

Do you remember the apostle Paul's ministry partner called Barnabas? His name was actually Joseph, but the nickname by which he was known means "Son of Encouragement" (Acts 4:36). What a compliment to give a person that label.

Barnabas encouraged the church in Jerusalem (Acts 4:36-37). He encouraged the new believers in Antioch (Acts 11:22). He was a constant encourager to Paul, such as the time he brought Paul along to work in Antioch (Acts 11:25-26). He was again an encourager to Paul by accompanying him on his first missionary journey (Acts 13:2-3). When Paul refused to take John Mark on a missionary journey because Mark had deserted him earlier, it was Barnabas who invited the young man along on another journey (Acts 15:37-41).

As Luke, the writer of the book of Acts, tells us, "Barnabas was a good man, full of the Holy Spirit and strong in faith. And many people were brought to the Lord" (Acts 11:24).

Did you get that? Barnabas was an encourager. The work of the Holy Spirit was evident in his life. He was strong in the faith. And because of his Spirit-filled encouragement, many people became followers of Christ.

When you write your note, simply offer words of encouragement. My letter to the family that owns the garbage pickup service was simply one of encouragement. I wanted them to know that I noticed the little things they did that made their service exemplary.

Your letter doesn't have to be long. In fact, brevity may be best. A few sentences of encouragement go a long way.

If you're aware of specific areas in the person's life where some encouragement may be helpful, include that in your letter. Part of the purpose in writing is to be a Barnabas to the recipient.

WHAT SHOULD I EXPECT?

Write your letter with no expectation of a response. Your purpose in writing is not to get a letter in return lauding your efforts for writing the letter. I heard a church member complain because she had written a letter of encouragement but had never heard back from the person. Your motive in writing should be unconditional encouragement, not to receive something in return.

Let God handle the response. The recipient may not know how to respond appropriately. He or she may have mixed-up priorities. He or she might be going through personal pain and not have the emotional stamina to respond. That's okay. You are writing a letter of grace and encouragement.

Above all, your letter is a letter of love. Take a moment and read 1 Corinthians 13:4-7. Love is others-focused instead of self-focused. It's all about how we can help and serve the other person.

Are you ready to write your letter, send your text, or type your email? Remember, it doesn't have to be long. I encourage you to write it as soon as possible so you won't put it off.

Right before you put the letter in the mailbox or hit send

for the text or email, say a prayer. Pray that God will use your words to make a big difference in the life of the recipient. Pray that God will be glorified in this letter, text, or email.

Now, it's time to write your letter.

Sign and date here when you have completed the eleventh day of the thirty-day challenge to become a Great Commission Christian.

Name: ....

Date: ....

TO BE UNASHAMED

I remember seeing the hurt on my mom's face. It is a pain that still upsets me to recall.

When I was growing up, the word *punk* referred to a generally younger person with more attitude and mouth than brains or common sense. And when I was fourteen, I was a punk.

A small group of my friends and I got together on a somewhat regular basis at two of the guys' homes. I'm not sure why we started gathering at those two homes to the exclusion of others, but that's what generally happened.

One day, my mom suggested that I invite all my friends to *our* house. It only seemed right to her that she should share the load of providing a place with snacks. I replied in no uncertain terms that I did not want my friends at our house. Naturally, my mom asked the obvious question: "Why not?"

"Because you embarrass me," I said. That's when I saw the look of pain on her face. That's when I saw the single tear in the corner of her eye. That's when I knew I was a punk.

Mom never mentioned it again. She never held it against me either. And she never again asked me to invite my friends to our house.

I had the best of intentions to apologize to my mother, especially after I reached adulthood. But I never did. Then came the dreaded phone call from my brother.

"Mom died."

It was sudden and unexpected. I had been with her for most of the day that she died. But no one knew it would be her last.

I never told her I was sorry.

I never told her how wrong I was to be ashamed of her.

TO BE ASHAMED OF JESUS

Jesus had tough and unfiltered words about being ashamed of him: "If anyone is ashamed of me and my message, the Son of Man will be ashamed of that person when he returns in his glory and in the glory of the Father and the holy angels" (Luke 9:26). The verse needs little commentary. If you are ashamed of Jesus, he will be ashamed of you.

For Day 12, let's focus on one passage of Scripture. Let's understand it well. More importantly, let's live it well. Our passage is Romans 1:16-17: "For I am not ashamed of this Good News about Christ. It is the power of God at work, saving everyone who believes—the Jew first and also the Gentile. This Good News tells us how God makes us right in his sight. This is accomplished from start to finish by faith. As the Scriptures say, 'It is through faith that a righteous person has life.'"

It's a powerful passage. And it is unambiguous in its declaration and meaning. As in the earlier passage where Jesus said we must not be ashamed of him, this passage is the apostle Paul's response. He declares powerfully and simply, "I am not ashamed of this Good News about Christ.

Take this twelfth day of the thirty-day challenge to focus on these two verses. First, make certain you are clear on its meaning. Second, begin thinking of its application in your life. What does it mean to not be ashamed of Christ and his Good News?

When you are unashamed of Christ, you want to get to know him better. You desire to study the Word of God more deeply. You want to converse with him more frequently in prayer. You want to talk about him to fellow believers who are also excited about Christ. You want to embrace Christ totally for your life.

When you are unashamed of Christ, you are eager to tell unbelievers about him. We call it evangelism. Unfortunately, stereotypes of evangelism abound. It is the person on a street corner declaring that everyone is going to hell. It is that person who shows up at your home uninvited and unwelcomed. It is that person who wants to corner you every day with his or her own superiority and smugness.

Real evangelism, however, is as natural and enthusiastic as grandparents telling people about their grandchildren. If you are a grandparent, you are not likely ashamed of your grandchildren. To the contrary, you likely overflow with joy thinking about them and talking about them.

UNASHAMED OF THE NARROW WAY OF CHRIST

Jesus was clear that the way of salvation is a narrow way. When he preached the Sermon on the Mount, he said, "You can enter God's Kingdom only through the narrow gate. The highway to hell is broad, and its gate is wide for the many who choose that way. But the gateway to life is very narrow and the road is difficult, and only a few ever find it" (Matthew 7:13-14).

In Romans 1:16-17, our focus text for today, the Good News of Christ is described as "the power of God at work, saving everyone who believes." Paul affirmed that the way of Christ is the only way, and it provides salvation to everyone who believes, indicating that belief in Christ is the narrow gate or way.

Paul further says in the passage that belief in Christ is

the only way "God makes us right in his sight." We are condemned sinners until we place our faith in Christ and receive both his forgiveness and his righteousness.

I get it. Many people in our culture today resist any declaration that there is only one God and one way. From their perspective, it seems narrow-minded and exclusionary. But here is the reality of the Good News of Christ: It *is* a narrow way, but it is *not* narrow-minded. It *is* exclusive, but it is *not* exclusionary. Jesus said: "I am the way, the truth, and the life. No one can come to the Father except through me" (John 14:6). But "*everyone* who calls on the name of the LORD will be saved" (Romans 10:13, italics added).

We are unashamed of Jesus. And we are unashamed to declare that he is the only way of salvation.

FROM START TO FINISH

In Christ, we are made right with God. Jesus went to the cross as our substitute so that we could be freely given that righteousness. But read Romans 1:17 closely, where Paul says, "This [righteousness] is accomplished from start to finish by faith."

Did you get that? Jesus is not only our salvation at a point in time, but his righteousness also stays with us our entire lives as we enter eternity. He is with us and never leaves us. He is not ashamed of us. We must not be ashamed of him.

Your assignment on Day 12 is basic but profound. Focus on Romans 1:16-17. Read it several times. Perhaps ask God in prayer to give you clarity about the verses for your life. And then ask yourself, "Am I ashamed of Christ?"

You can best answer the question by looking in the mirror. Do you talk about Christ with unbridled enthusiasm? Are you willing to defend him when his name is mocked or held in scorn? Are you living the life he has asked you to live without reservation?

And, finally, are you willing, even eager, to share the Good News of Christ with those who are not believers in him? If not, are you willing to begin praying for God to give you the courage, the words, and the love to share his Good News with others?

Sign and date here when you have completed the twelfth day of the thirty-day challenge to become a Great Commission Christian.

Name: ....

Date: ....

THE POWER OF THE INVITATION

Do you ever wonder what it was like to be in the presence of Jesus while he lived on earth?

Have you ever read some of the events recorded in Matthew, Mark, Luke, and John and wondered what was going on in the minds of the disciples and others who were in Christ's presence?

I do. But I probably don't have a sufficient imagination to get close to what they thought and felt.

But I still wonder.

One of the early events where my imagination goes into overdrive is when Jesus calls the first disciples to follow him. Matthew's record of it is succinct, leaving a lot to the imagination. Jesus first called Peter and Andrew: "One day as Jesus was walking along the shore of the Sea of Galilee, he saw two brothers—Simon, also called Peter, and Andrew—throwing a net into the water, for they fished for a living. Jesus called out to them, 'Come, follow me, and I will show you how to fish for people!' And they left their nets at once and followed him" (Matthew 4:18-20). What was going on in their minds when they heard that call? I wonder how well they really knew Jesus. I wonder what made them give up their livelihood immediately and follow him.

Jesus invited them to follow him. With a simple sentence of invitation, Jesus persuaded them to change their lives radically.

"A little farther up the shore" (Matthew 4:21), Jesus sees two more brothers. This time it is James and John. They are repairing their nets with their father, Zebedee. Jesus calls to them. And like Peter and Andrew, James and John drop everything and follow immediately.

I really wonder about all four of these early followers of Christ. In the second invitation, I wonder what poor Zebedee thought and did. He was likely depending on his sons to carry on the family business. They not only left their dad; they left him *immediately*. There was no discussion of succession or hiring someone to take their place. It was just, "We're out of here, Dad!" In my imagination, I see Zebedee holding a fishing net in his hand with his mouth agape.

In quick order, Jesus offered two powerful invitations.

Those invitations were life-altering. Even more, they shaped the eternal destinies of these early followers of his.

As a believer, you have responded to an invitation from Jesus. Though you did not see him visibly, you knew he was calling you to follow him. You may have been a young child. You may have followed him in your adult years. But your life was radically changed when you accepted his invitation. Your eternal destiny became heaven because you decided to follow him.

It is the power of the invitation.

NOW IT'S TIME FOR YOU TO INVITE

Jesus established a pattern for us to follow. We are to invite people into our lives. On this thirteenth day of the thirty-day challenge, you will be inviting people to church.

Why is the act of inviting so powerful? First, when you invite someone into your life or to your church, you are telling them that you care about them. Jesus invited Peter, Andrew, James, and John because he cared for them. He wanted them to experience the fullness of life that he offered. He wanted them to change the world with him.

We may assume that the natural default for those who are not believers or those not in church will be to say no to any invitation to church. That is simply not the case. Many years ago, I assembled a research team to investigate the attitudes of unchurched people in America (see my book *The Unchurched Next Door*). An amazing discovery we made was the high receptivity unchurched persons have to an invitation to church. In fact, three out of four indicated they would be receptive to an invitation to church.

Amazingly, the team found that only one out of twenty unchurched persons has an antagonistic attitude toward Christians and churches. Most people were not boycotting church because they didn't like Christians. They simply weren't going to church because they had never been invited.

Jesus talked about the reality of reaching people. He made it clear that the problem was not the availability of people to reach; it was the scarcity of those willing to reach them: "The harvest is great, but the workers are few. So pray to the Lord who is in charge of the harvest; ask him to send more workers into his fields" (Matthew 9:37-38).

Second, inviting someone to church is a Great Commission activity. Those you invite will likely hear the gospel or they will see the gospel in action among the church members. When you invite someone, you are inviting them to both a church service and an opportunity to hear and see the gospel.

Third, when you invite someone, you are taking the first step, or another step, toward befriending them. You are letting them know they matter to you.

I am challenging you to invite someone to church.

Indeed, by the time you get to Day 30, I will have challenged you to invite eight different people to church. If you have any doubts or anxiety about this challenge, you can relax. We have seen thousands of church members take this challenge. They have all seen great results when they've taken three key steps.

THE THREE STEPS OF AN EFFECTIVE CHURCH INVITATION

At the risk of stating the obvious, step one is taking the initiative. You first have to ask someone to join you at church. The invitation may take place in the office, at school, where a merchant works (I just invited my barber to my church), or in your neighborhood. The invitation may be extended by phone, by email, or in person. But you must actually invite someone.

Second, if you want to increase the chances that the person will accept your invitation, offer to walk into the church building together. Many people have a level of anxiety about entering a new place, especially a church. Your offer could go a long way toward relieving much of that anxiety.

Third, if you want the greatest probability of a positive response, invite the person to also go with you for a meal after the service. Barring some unforeseen circumstances, they are very likely to say yes.

Start thinking about the most natural and comfortable way for you to invite someone to church. Make a commitment to invite your first person before the week is over. You will have two more people to invite before the thirty-day challenge is over, so don't put it off more than a few days.

As always, pray for a name to come to your mind if you have not already done so. Once you have the name, pray for the person, couple, or family to be receptive to your invitation. After you have prayed, give yourself a deadline to make the invitation. Make certain the deadline is just a few days away.

By the way, the challenge for today is simply *inviting* someone to church. It does not necessarily mean the person will say yes. I pray they will, but your role is *obedience*. Your role is inviting someone.

Leave the results up to God.

Sign and date here when you have completed the thirteenth day of the thirty-day challenge to become a Great Commission Christian.

Name: ....

Date: ....

PRAYING FOR YOUR PASTOR AGAIN

It has been ten days since you first prayed for your pastor. Pastors need prayer consistently. Let's look at some more reasons why prayer is so important.

James is a pastor in Tennessee. He has served his church for nine years. Like any church, his congregation is a mixed bag of blessings and challenges. He deeply loves the members. He expresses and demonstrates that love often.

The day I spoke with James was one of those challenging days for him. He told me the story of Rick and how he had come to the church five years ago.

"Rick and his wife were close to divorce," Pastor James told me. "I spent hours counseling both of them. I referred them to a marriage counselor as well. It was a time-consuming endeavor, but it was worth the effort. The marriage made it. I was incredibly grateful for a number of reasons, but particularly because they had three children under eight years old."

James mentioned how he had invested countless hours mentoring Rick over the next few years.

"I spent more time with Rick than any other church member. Again, I counted my time with him as a great investment, a blessing worthy of the effort."

Then James began to speak slowly.

"Rick started attending church less frequently about a year ago. I would text or call him fairly regularly, but he became less responsive. Then, about two weeks ago, he emailed me to tell me that he and his family were moving to another church because they weren't getting fed at our church."

The pastor was crushed. Rick had never given any indication that he was unhappy at the church. He even called James his best friend. And now he was gone. The one person the pastor had given the most time to was gone. In ministry, that's sometimes how things go.

THE PASTOR'S ROLLER COASTER

In the course of a week, a pastor might celebrate a person becoming a follower of Christ, deal with a tragic suicide, receive an encouraging note, lead a contentious business meeting, rejoice at the birth of a child, and receive a hateful and anonymous letter of criticism. It's an emotional roller coaster.

When someone asks me if they should become a pastor, I respond, "Only if you absolutely know you have been called by God. You should not even think of doing it in your own power."

THE 24/7 JOB

Pastors hear regularly, "I would love your job. You only work one hour a week." Though the oft-repeated lines are meant to be funny, most pastors find little humor in them. They know that many people see their work as light and undemanding. To the contrary, most pastors work long and often weary hours. They take little time off.

In a Church Answers survey of pastors, many said they had interrupted a family vacation to return home to lead a funeral. Some pastors expressed deep regret for this because their wife and children were deeply hurt. Many pastors are torn between caring for their church members and taking time off with their families.

Some church members want pastors to spend more time doing counseling. Others want them visiting nursing homes, shut-in members, and hospitals. Some members expect pastors to connect with unchurched people several hours every week. Still other members demand their pastor keep forty hours per week of office hours, pushing visitation and other responsibilities to "after hours." Earlier I mentioned a pastor who told me that he had spoken with a pastoral search committee member who told him to anticipate working 120 hours a week.

Not surprisingly, he didn't take the job.

In most cases, the work expectations of pastors are high. If a church has two hundred members, the pastor has two hundred people who think he works for them. And that doesn't include the expectations of people outside the church.

THE SERMON AND PASTORS

In a study we conducted several years ago, our research team found that pastors of mostly healthy churches spent about twenty hours per week in sermon preparation (see my book *Surprising Insights from the Unchurched*). Keep in mind, those hours are above and beyond all the expectations noted thus far.

For sure, pastors need blocks of uninterrupted time to prepare sermons, but it doesn't always work that way. In fact, it rarely works that way. Some major interruption will take place. It may be as insignificant as someone dropping by to chat, or it may be the unexpected death of a faithful member of the church. Still, the pastor must get the sermon prepared.

Think about it. Pastors not only have to prepare a sermon every week, but most pastors also have to prepare around fifty sermons a year. The ministry is never-ending. The challenges are always there.

FOR YOU TO KNOW

So why have I given you this brief overview of the challenges of being a pastor? Simply stated, I want you to know how to pray for your pastor. If you and your church are to become vehicles of Great Commission obedience, your pastor needs to lead the way. And your pastor needs strength, wisdom, and God's protection. You need to pray for all of these and more for your pastor.

A Great Commission church is usually led by a Great Commission pastor. Church members follow the lead of a Great Commission pastor. But the enemy will do anything in his circumscribed power to hinder a pastor's work. Such is the reason prayer is so vital.

A FEW AREAS FOR PRAYER

Of course, you can feel free to pray for your pastor in any direction you are led. Let me suggest a few areas that pastors mention the most.

Pray for wisdom for your pastor. The decisions pastors must make are numerous. Some are minor. Some are of major consequence.

Pray for your pastor to have the right priorities. Because of the constant requests and demands that pastors receive, they often respond to the most vocal demand rather than the ones of greatest importance.

Pray for your pastor's family. Spouses and children often feel the burden of being a part of a pastor's family. They often sense the eyes of those looking in the glass house. And many of them are hurt and lonely.

Pray for your pastor's sermons. This includes sermon preparation time as well as the actual delivery of the sermon. More people see and hear the pastor in this relatively short period than at any other time of the week.

Pray for your pastor's emotional, physical, and spiritual stamina. The work of a pastor's ministry is demanding, and it can be exhausting. Pastors who are tired are pastors who may get into trouble.

Pray for your pastor's Great Commission leadership. For sure, we are taking these thirty days to challenge you personally to be a Great Commission Christian. But God intended for Christians to do most of their ministry in the local church. You will be a stronger Great Commission Christian if your church is committed to evangelism. Your church will be a stronger Great Commission church if your pastor is committed to evangelism too. Such is the primary reason we are asking you to pray for your pastor today. By the way, there is nothing wrong with praying for your pastor every day!

Sign and date here when you have completed the fourteenth day of the thirty-day challenge to become a Great Commission Christian.

Name: ....

Date: ....

IT'S TIME TO GO

"It's time to go."

I remember those four words well: My dad may have said them on other occasions, but I remember them best when we took our family vacations.

There was no variety to our family vacations. We always went to Panama City Beach. It was always in July. Always for two weeks. Always at the same motel. We loved the emerald water and the sugar-white sand. In those days, development was modest, and we had twenty-foot sand dunes on the beach. We loved Florida.

I still love Florida.

On one occasion, my mom convinced my dad to try

something different. That year, we went to Texas. But after a few days there, we all changed our minds and made the long drive to Panama City Beach.

"It's time to go."

I love those four words for another reason, a reason more important than a family vacation. Those words summarize what Jesus told us to do.

"Hey, Christians, it's time to go."

Of course, he gave a few more instructions at the time: "Therefore, go and make disciples of all the nations, baptizing them in the name of the Father and the Son and the Holy Spirit" (Matthew 28:19).

On another occasion he said, "You will receive power when the Holy Spirit comes upon you. And you will be my witnesses, telling people about me everywhere—in Jerusalem, throughout Judea, in Samaria, and to the ends of the earth" (Acts 1:8).

Jesus didn't just remind us; he commanded us to go. The first part of Matthew 28:19 could be translated like this: "*As you are going*, make disciples of all the nations" (italics added). Indeed, Jesus expected us to be in a continuous process of going. He makes a similar point in Acts 1:8 when he commands his disciples to be witnesses in four expanding geographical areas.

Now it's time for *you* to go. Simply stated, you can't stand still and be a Great Commission Christian.

THE SIMPLE ACT OF GOING

For Day 15, go into your neighborhood and pray for ten different families.

But first, let me explain how easy it will be.

Choose a group of houses near your home. Either walk or drive there. Just start walking and praying for each house you pass. You can walk slowly or stop briefly in front of each home. After you've prayed for ten homes, you're done.

Now let's expand it a bit.

First, you need to be safe. If for any reason you feel unsafe walking in a neighborhood, stay in your car and pray as you pass each home. Even better, get someone to go with you. If you live in a rural area, it might not be practical to walk. That's okay, you can pray just fine in your car.

Second, your prayer for each home can be brief—even under a minute. Ask the Holy Spirit to guide your thoughts and pray for the things that come to mind. The purpose of this challenge is to get you out into the community and praying for other people.

Third, you are not expected to talk to anyone. If the Holy Spirit opens up an opportunity, by all means take it. But this challenge is simply to get you going and praying.

WHAT DO I PRAY?

Can you really pray a meaningful prayer in a minute? The content of your prayers is more important than the duration.

Even a minute is long enough to pray for a few areas for each home. Here are some examples.

Pray for those in each home to be aware of God's presence in their lives. You may not know the specific needs in each home, but praying for an awareness of God's presence is always a good place to start. We received a report at Church Answers about a woman with advanced cancer who decided to come to church "out of the blue." She was in one of the homes where church members had prayed. She later became a follower of Christ and cancer-free!

Pray for those in each home to become followers of Christ. This prayer should be a top priority. Of course, some people will already be Christians, but many will not. It is an incredible blessing to see how the Holy Spirit works as we pray.

Pray for those in each home to get involved in a church. The pattern of the New Testament is clear. It is God's plan for Christians to get connected to a local church. Most of the New Testament, after the four Gospels, is about the local church, or letters to a local church leader or a local church congregation. God's plan is for the local church—and he didn't leave us a plan B.

Of course, you can pray in many other directions as the Holy Spirit guides you. However you choose to pray, the point is to get out there and get started today.

AN ADDED ELEMENT

In our ministry package called Pray & Go (PrayAndGoChurch. com), we add the element of a door hanger to this Great Commission prayer effort. After praying for those in a home, you leave a door hanger to let them know you prayed for them. The door hanger typically provides information to contact the church if the people would like to write to you or talk with you.

Some Christians have used a card, like a business card, instead of a door hanger. Either one works fine for letting people know you prayed for them. But heed this word of caution: Do not put the card or hanger *in* or *on* the mailbox. It is prohibited in most communities, and it's not a good witness in any case.

We also recommend that you note the addresses of the homes where you have prayed. As you will see on later days of this thirty-day challenge, you will be going into your community three more times. Perhaps you will be inspired and motivated to make this effort an integral part of your spiritual disciplines. Over several months, it will be exciting to see how many homes and other places you've prayed for.

PRAY BEFORE YOU GO . . .

This is the first of four challenges that will get you out into your community. We have heard remarkable and inspiring testimonies from church members who have made the commitment to go and pray.

Here's a vital piece that I want to emphasize: *Pray before you go.*

We call our resource Pray & Go because we encourage those walking into their communities to pray for their efforts before they leave. Pray first, then go. Pray for open hearts in the homes. Pray for safety. Pray for your own witness. Pray for God to give you the right words if you do engage someone in a conversation.

Prayer walking is such a simple exercise, but don't let the simplicity lead you to believe that God can't use your efforts in profound ways. We have been helping Christians and churches get out into their communities for years, and we never cease to be amazed at the way God honors these efforts.

Even as I write these words, I am praying for *you.* Chances are I don't know you, but I am thankful for you. Indeed, I am thankful that you care about others and their relationship with Jesus Christ.

Sign and date here when you have completed the fifteenth day of the thirty-day challenge to become a Great Commission Christian.

Name: ....

Date: ....

VIP: VERY IMPORTANT PRAYERS

Congratulations on completing the first fifteen days of this thirty-day challenge. Many of the days have been dedicated to prayer because we simply cannot separate prayer from the Great Commission. We seek to *go* in God's power, not our own.

Thus, we will take Day 16 to pray again for several important people and issues. This day is both a summary and a review, but it's also more. We are praying for some very important matters. They are worthy of our attention.

PRAY FOR AN OUTWARDLY FOCUSED HEART

We began this thirty-day challenge with a prayer for an out-wardly focused heart. Obedience to the Great Commission is a matter of the heart. It is a matter of obedience.

Jesus told us that our treasures are a reflection of the desires of our heart: "Wherever your treasure is, there the desires of your heart will also be" (Matthew 6:21). If you ask most Christians what their treasure is, I would be surprised if many mentioned the Great Commission. Our prayer again today is that God would give us a desire to reach beyond ourselves.

We become committed to those areas of life that excite us the most. While there is nothing wrong with getting excited about a sports team, a hobby, or a trip to the beach, we can pray that God will give us a renewed excitement to be obedient to the Great Commission.

Pray again today that God will help you turn your focus outward.

PRAY FOR AN OUTWARDLY FOCUSED CHURCH

Pray again for your church to become outwardly focused. Perhaps this time as you are praying for your congregation, you can think of specific members for whom to pray. Some of your fellow members work in places where they interact with non-Christians on a regular basis. They are in the middle of a great mission field.

Other church members you know have a specific sphere of influence. Take Jamie for example. When I met her at a conference where I was speaking, she told me she was "just a stay-at-home mom." My message that day had focused on encouraging people to share the gospel within their spheres of influence. But Jamie didn't think she had a sphere of influence—apart from the obviously important influence she had on her children.

As we talked further, we somehow got on the subject of her neighborhood homeowners association. She was the chair of the landscaping committee and worked with dozens of her neighbors. The moment she told me about it, the light went on in her mind.

"Wow!" she exclaimed. "I do have a sphere of influence! That's my mission field!"

You likely have a number of fellow church members who don't realize they have spheres of influence. Pray for them to discover their mission fields.

PRAY FOR YOUR PASTOR

Go back to Days 4 and 14. Look at the descriptions of a typical pastor's life. Remind yourself again of the challenges pastors face in the midst of the victories they celebrate.

May I make a suggestion at this point? Write a brief email to your pastor. Tell him about your thirty-day commitment and how you have already been praying for him. Even better, tell him you plan to pray for him regularly beyond the thirty days.

I know you will encourage your pastor. I know such

emails lift pastors' spirits and give them God-blessed motivation to press on in ministry. Usually, happy church members don't write and encourage their pastors. But unhappy and critical church members are very likely to complain. Surprise your pastor with a brief email of encouragement.

It will make all the difference in the world. It really will.

PRAY FOR THE POWER OF THE HOLY SPIRIT

I cannot imagine what it was like at Pentecost when the Holy Spirit first came upon the believers in Jerusalem. Jesus had told his followers that the Spirit would be coming shortly. He told them that the Holy Spirit would give them the power they needed to be witnesses: "You will receive power when the Holy Spirit comes upon you. And you will be my witnesses, telling people about me everywhere" (Acts 1:8).

Yes, Jesus told them. But did they really know what was coming? Could they have possibly anticipated that about three thousand people would be saved in one day? (Acts 2:41). Did they really think they would change the world?

Maybe not. But they *did*.

And you can too.

The Holy Spirit is the same as he was two thousand years ago. He is the same as he was at Creation.

You prayed for the power of the Holy Spirit on Day 6.

Pray again for that power. See what God will do through you and through your church.

PRAY FOR YOUR COMMUNITY

You live in your own Jerusalem. God has put you in your community for a reason. God has put you at your home address for a reason.

Pray again for your community. You could start by praying for the ten families that live closest to you. Even if you don't know the names of all of them, you can pray for them.

You have probably discovered already that God is opening doors for you as you completed the first half of your thirty-day challenge.

Wouldn't it be great if it became clearly evident that God is using you to reach your neighbors and your community?

Pray with boldness and with confidence that you will indeed be a witness in your community.

Watch God open doors in miraculous ways.

PRAY FOR OBEDIENCE

Again, pray for your own obedience. This thirty-day challenge is, well, a challenge. You know you have been given commands and commissions to be a Great Commission

Christian. The only way you can argue with that truth is to argue with the words of Jesus.

You know that Jesus clearly said he is the only way of salvation. If you ever waver on that truth, read John 14:6. Jesus did not mince words. He said he is the only way, the only truth, and the only life. And he said that no one can come to the Father except through him.

It's a powerful message. And it's an exclusive message. You have been called to be a bearer of that message. We call it the Good News because it is the best news ever. God loves us so much that he sent his Son to die for us. To forgive our sins. To provide the only path to heaven.

Pray that you will be obedient to share that Good News faithfully and regularly.

PRAY FOR YOUR ONE

On Day 10, you began praying for your one, a person who is not in church and is likely not a believer in Christ. Let this day be a reminder to keep praying for your one. As you pray for him or her, take careful note of how God opens doors for you to connect with your one.

As I write these words, my one is a hair stylist named Kristen. She has been cutting my hair for more than a year. We began to have spiritual conversations pretty quickly as she shared with me concerns and needs for her family.

I have shared the gospel with her. I invited her and her husband to church and then lunch after the service. She finally accepted. I am praying for my one that she will respond to the gospel. She seems so close, so very close.

Indeed, I hope by the time you have read these words, Kristen will be a follower of Christ. She is my one, but I am praying she will be one who belongs to Jesus.

Keep praying for your one.

Sign and date here when you have completed the sixteenth day of the thirty-day challenge to become a Great Commission Christian.

Name: ....

Date: ....

WRITE TO SOMEONE AGAIN

On Day 11, you wrote your first outwardly focused letter. You likely tried to be an encourager in the biblical model of Barnabas. It's time to write another letter.

Let's take a moment to remember why you are writing these letters.

First, it has become clear that you are to be an encourager. Everyone needs encouragement. Everyone needs a positive word from time to time. It is exciting that you are able to be that conduit of encouragement and joy to someone.

Second, you are to be a source of comfort. Everyone hurts at times. Many people hurt a lot of the time. It is likely the person to whom you are writing is in the midst of some struggle or some pain. Your note to them may come at God's perfect time.

Several years ago, I found myself in a leadership crisis I never could have expected. Indeed, I heard things said about me I never would have imagined. Even though the negative words were not true, they still hurt. They hurt a lot.

Then I received a text from Steve, a friend but not necessarily someone I knew well. The text read, "None of us believes what they are saying about you, Thom. Your integrity and character will prevail. We know the real Thom Rainer."

God's timing was perfect. The message was perfect. At that point, I knew I would see the other side with victory. It would be several weeks before the crisis passed, but it did pass. And though it still hurts at times to think about it, I really have moved on. The world has moved on. I am indeed on the other side of that painful time in my life.

And I will never forget Steve's text. I will never forget how he was an incredible source of comfort. I'm glad I took the time later to let him know what his words meant to me.

It was a brief message. It was a simple text.

But it was life-changing for me.

Now, it's your time to minister to someone.

But there's a third reason why I'm asking you to write another letter, email, or text. The primary purpose of these thirty days is to get you focused beyond yourself. We all tend to become inwardly focused. God's plan is for us to look, serve, and go beyond ourselves. Believe it or not, the simple act of writing to someone does just that.

TO WHOM DO YOU WRITE THIS TIME?

As you likely have noticed by now, this thirty-day challenge doesn't have firmly fixed prescriptions for each day. There is flexibility in how you meet each day's challenge. There is flexibility so the Holy Spirit can lead us without a script getting in the way. The same rules apply today. Prayerfully decide the best way forward.

By the way, I'm taking this challenge with you. Before starting this chapter, I prayed that God would bring some people to mind who could use some comfort and encouragement. I will note a few of those people whose names surfaced after I prayed.

My cousin lost her husband to a heart attack over a year ago. She obviously still struggles.

One of my closer friends had to admit his wife for long-term dementia care. He is so devoted to her, but she no longer recognizes him.

A couple in my community group at church bought land for their dream home. But home prices have escalated so much and so rapidly that they can no longer afford to build.

My son Art is starting a new business this month. He left the security of a regular paycheck to follow his dream.

Another close friend is waiting on tests for his son who was in remission from a rare form of cancer. The tests may show that the cancer has returned. The son has three young sons of his own.

Just a moment ago, I looked at a social media feed and saw that a friend was struggling with depression.

These six needs came to my mind right after I prayed. I immediately called one of these people and texted two more. There is no shortage of people who need comfort and encouragement.

All six of the people I noted here are Christians. But there's no reason to limit ourselves if we want to become Great Commission Christians. Yesterday, I prayed for God to connect me with someone who is not a Christian. God could not have been clearer in his answer to my prayer. I ran into a lady in the parking lot where my office is located. She's been asking many spiritual questions. I pray that God will continue to use me to encourage her and witness to her.

To whom will you write this time? What words can you offer to comfort someone or encourage someone? Though the assignment is brief, it can be incredibly powerful.

DON'T FORGET THE PRINCIPLE OF THE HARVEST

If you asked a few Christians to describe Jesus' teaching on the harvest, I bet that some would respond that Jesus told us to pray for lost people. Though it is certainly important to pray for people who are not yet Christians, that wasn't what Jesus focused on in addressing the harvest.

Let's review his words from Matthew 9:36-38: "When he saw the crowds, he had compassion on them because they were confused and helpless, like sheep without a shepherd. He said to his disciples, 'The harvest is great, but the workers are few. So pray to the Lord who is in charge of the harvest; ask him to send more workers into his fields.'"

Did you get that? There is no shortage of people to reach. Quite frankly, there is no shortage of people who would be open to a text, email, or conversation from you. We sometimes convince ourselves that people will resist any overtures on our part. That simply isn't true; it never has been true. The harvest is great. We need more *workers* in the field.

You, my friend, are a worker in the field. Your prayers, your emails, your texts, your invitations, and your conversations are all part of what a worker in the field does. Your obedience is making a difference. You are one of God's workers who are changing the world.

SEE WHAT GOD DOES

My friend whose son is facing a possible recurrence of cancer answered my call immediately. We talked for several minutes.

We prayed. And we both knew that we will always be there for each other.

I texted another friend, who also responded immediately. His words spoke volumes about his need and his hurt. His text simply read, "Thanks, Thom. I needed this touch just now."

The other friend I texted has not responded, but it's only been thirty minutes. I have no doubt we will connect with each other before the day is over.

I offer these examples to encourage you to take action, to write to someone in your sphere of influence today. I want you to realize how great the potential harvest really is. I want you to see how God works powerfully—and often quickly—in response to our obedience.

Are you ready to write your letter, email, or text? Pray a brief prayer for God's blessing as you send it. I am also praying for you.

It's your time. Be a faithful worker in the harvest field.

Sign and date here when you have completed the seventeenth day of the thirty-day challenge to become a Great Commission Christian.

Name: ....

Date: ....

PRAYING FOR UNITY

A thriving church had two great initiatives underway. First, the congregation had become outwardly focused. They were "praying and going" much like you did on Day 15. Second, they were remodeling major portions of their church facilities. They knew the old buildings were not adequate for the post-pandemic world.

There was a lot of excitement. Participation was high. Growth was occurring every week.

Then it stopped.

The pastors and elders called our team for a consultation. They were almost desperate to find out what had happened. How could something so positive stop dead in its tracks? It didn't take our team long to discover the problem.

The church was reconfiguring its worship center and foyer. They needed a larger welcome center, so they reduced the worship seating capacity from five hundred to four hundred. It was a needed change. The church's average attendance was up to three hundred, but they were in two services. They had plenty of space. As the church continued to grow, they could add more services. The larger foyer or welcome center was the priority.

In our interviews with church members, we heard a lot of excitement about the Pray & Go initiative. But for those more involved in the renovation project, the attitude was almost the opposite. Those members were discouraged. A few were even angry.

The main sticking point was the remodeling of the worship center. The old pews had been removed. The church was meeting in the family life center during the construction. But a decision had to be made for the renovated worship center: pews or chairs?

No one anticipated the strong emotions that resulted. In fact, the controversy became known as "the pews versus chairs" argument. There were members with strong feelings on both sides.

In the meantime, the growth of the church came to a standstill. The steady flow of guests stopped almost completely. The feeling of unity had been replaced by an atmosphere of contention. One church member said it succinctly:

"The change in the attitude seemed like it happened overnight. We went from a growing church to a fighting church."

JESUS ON UNITY: FIGHTING THE EVIL ONE

On the night that he was betrayed, Jesus prayed a powerful
prayer of unity to the Father. It was obviously heard by his
followers, because John recorded his words. As Jesus prayed,
he uttered these telling words: "I'm not asking you to take
them out of the world, but to keep them safe from the evil
one" (John 17:15).

In the context in which Jesus prayed these words, he was
praying for unity among his followers. He was praying that
they would all be singularly focused on the mission he had
given them. But he knew that Satan, called the evil one,
would do everything in his power to distract the followers of
Christ and destroy their unity.

Before "the pews versus chairs" argument erupted, the
congregation had been on mission for Christ. They were
going into neighborhoods and praying for the families in
their homes. Many of those families had started visiting the
church. Some had become followers of Christ. The energy in
the church was palpable. But then the spiritual momentum
stopped.

The evil one will try to stop Great Commission obedience
and activity. For a season, he succeeded. The people started

fighting over pews and chairs. Their spiritual and emotional energy became focused on an incredibly trivial matter. Church members were more concerned about their seating arrangement than seeing people become followers of Christ.

I'm sure you get the point by now. As you pray for unity in the church, pray for protection from the enemy. Jesus specifically prayed that his followers would be kept safe from Satan.

That should be our prayer as well. That should be your prayer right now.

JESUS ON UNITY: THE SPECIFIC PRAYER

Jesus continued his prayer to the Father, this time with a specific emphasis on unity: "I am praying not only for these disciples but also for all who will ever believe in me through their message. I pray that they will all be one, just as you and I are one—as you are in me, Father, and I am in you. And may they be in us so that the world will believe you sent me" (John 17:20-21).

A fascinating aspect of this passage is that Jesus prays for his immediate disciples, who were there with him in the upper room. But he also prays for all future believers—"for all who will ever believe in me through their message."

That part of the prayer is breathtaking. Jesus is praying for our unity right now. He is praying for our churches to be unified today. He looked across time and space and saw us in our churches right now. And he prayed that we would be one, that we would be unified.

JESUS ON UNITY: THE REASON FOR THE PRAYER

Though it may seem self-evident why Jesus prayed this prayer for unity, he wants us to be certain we understand the importance of the matter. Read his words closely: "I am in them and you are in me. May they experience such perfect unity that the world will know that you sent me and that you love them as much as you love me" (John 17:23).

Did you get that? When Christians and churches are unified, unbelievers in the world will see the gospel in that unity. The world will know that God sent Jesus. The world will know that Jesus came to die for our sins. The world will know that God loves them so much that he sent his one and only Son to be a sacrifice for us.

You cannot be a Great Commission Christian and be at odds with other believers. You cannot be a Great Commission church and have infighting in the church.

Unity is imperative for the Great Commission.

YOUR PRAYER FOR UNITY

Today, you are asked to pray for unity for your church. I encourage you to begin by praying for your own attitude. Are you at odds with anyone else? Are you seeking to get your own way in the church rather than yielding to the preferences of others?

Then, pray for your entire church. If there are particular areas of disunity, pray for those needs with great specificity. If you don't know of any areas of disunity in your church, rejoice in the peace and joy that is present. And specifically pray that you and your fellow members will be protected from the wiles of the evil one. You can be certain that Satan will do anything and everything in his power to destroy the unity in your church.

This prayer may indeed be one of the most important prayers you pray during this thirty-day challenge. A church without unity is a church without the power of the Great Commission.

By the way, sometimes disunity happens more subtly than an overt conflict. In fact, Satan may be more successful at whispering distractions in our ears than precipitating arguments and overt conflict in the church. So pray for focus, for protection from distractions. Pray specifically that you and your fellow church members will not be drawn away from obedience to the Great Commission; that you will remain faithful to this thirty-day challenge.

Your involvement in this challenge is a form of spiritual warfare, taking the fight to the enemy. And one of the enemy's greatest countertactics is to try to distract or disunify your church.

Such is the reason you are praying for unity in your church right now.

Sign and date here when you have completed the eighteenth day of the thirty-day challenge to become a Great Commission Christian.

Name: ....

Date: ....

THE GREAT COMMISSION PASSAGE

You have seen the phrase *Great Commission* many times in this thirty-day challenge. It might be helpful, then, to examine a Great Commission passage from the Bible. If we are seeking to be Great Commission Christians, it behooves us to know exactly what the Great Commission is.

Although there is not a singularly definitive Scripture passage about the Great Commission, Matthew 28:18-20 is likely the best-known among several. It certainly is packed and comprehensive for only three verses. Let's review the passage again: "Jesus came and told his disciples, 'I have been given all authority in heaven and on earth. Therefore, go and make disciples of all the nations, baptizing them in the name of the Father and the Son and the Holy Spirit. Teach these new disciples to obey all the commands I have given you. And be sure of this: I am with you always, even to the end of the age.'"

Mark 16:15 is an abbreviated version of the Great Commission: "[Jesus] told them, 'Go into all the world and preach the Good News to everyone.'" We already looked at Acts 1:8 on Day 2. It is one of the most-often cited Great Commission verses. Luke 10:2 and Matthew 9:38 are similar to each other, in that Jesus implores believers to pray for workers to be sent into the harvest fields.

THE AUTHORITY FACTOR

My first job out of college was with a well-known bank in Atlanta. Though the bank has been through several mergers since my tenure there, it had a very solid reputation throughout the Southeast. When I would call on a prospective commercial customer, I often got immediate attention when I gave the person the name of my bank.

The bank's name had prestige, influence, and authority. Indeed, I took the job in part because of the bank's stellar reputation. It carried a lot of weight in the community.

Jesus reminds us that when we share the gospel, we do so under his authority: "I have been given all authority in heaven and on earth" (Matthew 28:18). The name of Jesus is the greatest name ever. When we witness, we are his ambassadors. Therefore, we carry his authority into our communities.

When you decided to take this thirty-day challenge, you may have wondered whether you could really do it. You may have thought you couldn't see yourself telling others about Jesus. You may have come with doubts that you could become a Great Commission Christian.

I get it. I've been through some of those same doubts myself. But when I realize that I *go* and *speak* with the authority of Jesus, my entire perspective changes. I gain confidence because my confidence is in Jesus.

The first time I intentionally shared the gospel with someone, I was so nervous and my words were so convoluted that I was sure I had totally blown it. But the friend to whom I was witnessing calmly told me he wanted to hear more. He became a believer in Christ that very day. That was not my power. That was not my authority. That was the authority and power of Jesus.

JESUS SAID "GO"

The command from Jesus is unequivocal: "Go and make disciples." The word *go* in the original language of the Gospels refers to more than a singular act of sharing the gospel. It could also be translated "*as* you are going." In other words, being a witness for Jesus is a continuous action and a continuous state of mind.

The implications of this command are significant. In

order to be in a continuous mode of going, we must be prepared. Such preparation should include praying for the right words, the right opportunity, and the eyes to see those opportunities. I cannot recall a time when I prayed for opportunities where God did not give me one in short order. In fact, I am usually surprised by how quickly the opportunities come.

Another implication of this command is that our lifestyle must reflect well on our verbal witness. We will not typically find a receptive audience if our behavior and actions contradict the life Christ intended for us to live.

Think about how far you have traveled in these first nineteen days. We began with basic prayers and study verses, and now we are talking about becoming an ongoing witness for Christ. Indeed, my prayer is that you will conclude this study with a new desire and a new confidence in Christ, that you will be a witness for him every day "as you are going."

THE POWER AND THE PRESENCE

Jesus said to go. Indeed, he said to continuously go. And he reminded us that, as we go, we are going under his authority. Such a statement is powerful. But the Great Commission encompasses even more.

Jesus also told us he would be *with* us as we go. When we become witnesses for Christ, he promises to be right there as we speak: "Be sure of this: I am with you always, even to the end of the age" (Matthew 28:20).

When I was a young teenager, I always wanted to hang out with a guy named Bill. He was my favorite friend at the time for several reasons. First, he had a driver's license because he was three years older than I was. Second, he had a car, a pretty nice car back in those days. Third, he was bigger than I was. When we went somewhere, such as to a ball game, he would remind me that he had my back.

When I walked with Bill, I walked with confidence, maybe even a bit of a swagger. I knew he would take care of me. I knew he was with me to protect me whenever we were together.

Now I realize I have much more than a bigger friend to protect me and be with me. I have Jesus, the King of kings and the Creator of the universe. He is with me. And he promises to be with me until the very end.

Jesus uttered these words as a reminder that we don't become Great Commission Christians in our own power. He reminded us that he is with us always. We have both his presence and his power when we share the gospel.

THE GREAT COMMISSION IS FOR US . . . TODAY

Though Jesus gave the Great Commission to his immediate eleven disciples in Matthew 28:18-20, he meant the words to carry to all Christians throughout the ages. Such is the reason he said he is with us "even to the end of the age."

Your study of this Great Commission passage for Day 19 should be a great encouragement to you. As we seek to become the Great Commission Christians that Jesus intends for us to be, his words remind us that we are not doing this mission on our own. We go in his authority. We go with his presence. And we go with confidence because he promised us he would be with us to the end of the age.

Make certain you have read Matthew 28:18-20 closely. Make sure you understand it fully. And pray that you will be obedient to the words that Jesus left us.

Sign and date here when you have completed the nineteenth day of the thirty-day challenge to become a Great Commission Christian.

Name: ....

Date: ....

PRAY AND GO FOR THE FAMILIES

When we look at the version of the Great Commission in Matthew 28:18-20, we see a clear command to *go*. In fact, we are reminded that witnessing for Christ means being evangelistic *as we go*.

It is time for you to begin your second mission of going. You were introduced to the concept of praying and going on Day 15. This mission is the same as it was on Day 15, but today I will guide you more specifically on how to pray for the people in the homes you pass.

Once again, the mission is simple. Go to ten homes in your neighborhood or community (different from the ten you prayed for before). As you pass each home, pause or walk slowly and pray for the residents. If you are walking in a neighborhood, you should be able to complete the mission in about thirty minutes.

Again, I exhort you to put safety first. You may need to pray from your car, especially if you live in a sparsely populated community. Still, it is best if you can walk the neighborhood. Walking puts you in close proximity to the homes of the people for whom you are praying.

As a reminder, the purpose of this mission is not to knock on doors or talk to people. It is simply to pray for the families in the homes as you walk by. Don't be surprised, though, if God provides you some unexpected opportunities to talk with people. Pray about that possibility before you go out so you'll be prepared.

In this second pray-and-go mission, we will focus on the *needs* of the families in the homes. Obviously, we cannot know what their needs are. We can, however, pray for categories of needs that are common to most people. Feel free to make adjustments to both the process and your prayers as you feel led.

PRAY FOR COUPLES

As a point of clarity, every category of prayer may not apply to every home. For example, as you pray for couples, there may not be a married couple in the home. The home could include a single person or single parent. Your role is simply to pray and to leave the precision and application of the prayer to God.

When you pray for couples, pray for the health of their relationship. Many couples are struggling. Some are considering separation or divorce. Many are hurting deeply. You may not know the names of those for whom you are praying, and they don't know that you're praying for them—unless you're using the door hanger option. But God knows that you're praying. Pray with the expectation that he will work in the couple's marriage.

Some homes will include couples whose marriages are relatively healthy, but who have upside-down priorities. Perhaps they are working too much or not spending enough time with their kids.

Pray for these couples. Your prayers may be brief, but they will be powerful.

PRAY FOR THE CHILDREN

Some of the homes may have children. The children may be young and the parents are feeling the stresses and strains of caring for the needs and demands of young kids. Or they might be teenagers, with all the challenges that age brings.

You might pray specifically for the teens, knowing that most are feeling some type of peer pressure. It would not be unusual for some to have gotten involved with drinking, drugs, or sex. Others may have self-doubts and wonder where their future lies. It could be that you will be praying for a family with a teenager contemplating suicide. Whatever the case, God knows the specifics. Pray faithfully and leave the results to him.

As you pass each home, pray for whatever children are living there. Pray for their protection. Pray that they will experience the love of God in their lives.

PRAY FOR THEIR HEALTH

A pastor friend of mine recently shared a pray-and-go experience from one of his church members. Natalie made a commitment to pray for five hundred homes in one month, and she was well on her way by the fifteenth. Because of her big commitment, she had to move fairly quickly from home to home.

Natalie was also leaving a door hanger at each home. The door hanger, as we noted earlier, let the occupants of the home know that someone had prayed for them. It also included contact information of Natalie's church and the text number and email address to make prayer requests.

As she was moving from home to home, she felt led to pray for the physical health of the people in one particular home. After Natalie left the door hanger, someone stepped outside and called to her. She turned around to see a woman beckoning her to return.

When Natalie got closer to the woman, she could see tears streaming down her face. Her name was Miriam. She almost immediately told Natalie about her terminal cancer. She said in short breaths that she had three young children. Her husband was devoted to her and the children, but she was devastated at the thought of leaving them.

Natalie did not make any more prayer visits that day. She spent the next hour listening to Miriam and praying for her. In fact, Natalie visited Miriam several more times in the weeks ahead. Each time, she would pray for her. Sometimes, she prayed for healing. Other times, she simply prayed that Miriam would have peace.

The greatest news is that both Miriam and her husband became followers of Christ. And though God chose not to heal Miriam physically, he did heal her spiritually and gave her the gift of eternal life.

Natalie was with Miriam on the day she died. Other than her family, she was the last person to tell her goodbye.

Pray for the physical needs of those in the homes you pass. You never know what needs are present.

PRAY FOR THEIR FINANCIAL NEEDS

My son Art is a leader in the world of Christian finance. Through his company, Christian Money Solutions, he sees how many families are struggling and hurting due to significant money problems. I recently spoke to a single mom who struggles to sleep because she worries about her financial situation.

As you walk by each of the ten homes, pray for wisdom, guidance, blessing, and relief for the finances of these families. Some people carry stress far beyond what we could imagine.

Obviously, financial struggles affect both marriages and children. Your prayers could affect a number of areas in their lives positively.

PRAY FOR THEIR SALVATION

The greatest need in every home is salvation through Jesus Christ. Most likely, there will be Christians in some of the homes, but your prayers will still not be in vain. We have a computer folder full of pray-and-go stories where people eventually became followers of Christ after someone prayed for the people in their home. It is incredibly rewarding to see how God answers these prayers almost every time a church encourages its members to pray and go.

If you leave a card or door hanger, make sure you leave information about the address of your church, the times of services, and contact information if they want someone to pray for a specific need. We rejoice every time we hear the story of someone who went to church after a church member prayed for their home.

In many cases, those who visit an outwardly focused, pray-and-go church soon become followers of Christ themselves. That is a powerful example of what can happen when we become Great Commission Christians.

Sign and date here when you have completed the twentieth day of the thirty-day challenge to become a Great Commission Christian.

Name: ....

Date: ....

INVITE YOUR THREE

On Day 13, you invited someone to church. I wish I were able to hear about the invitation you made. I'm curious: Were you nervous or uncertain? How did the person respond? Were they friendly? Did they seem offended by the invitation? How did you feel after you made the invitation? Are you more or less eager to invite someone again?

This time, you will invite three people. Again, the method of invitation is up to you. But don't forget how powerful the simple act of inviting someone is. It shows you care. You are attempting to enhance a relationship. You will at least cause someone to think about connecting with a body of believers.

I wouldn't be surprised that some of your invitees have already shown up for church. They are likely being exposed to the gospel in the preaching, teaching, and Christian fellowship—which could be eye-opening for them if they are not yet Christians. We have heard numerous stories about church members who intentionally invited people to church and soon saw those people become Christians.

Think about it for a moment. Your invitation is an act of eternal significance. It is so simple, yet so profound. Please don't take today's assignment lightly. Indeed, never take the act of inviting people to church lightly.

Again, I encourage you to pray before you send the invitations. Pray that God will use your words to prepare the person for your invitation.

You might already have three names in mind. But if you're struggling about whom to invite, here are some suggestions.

CHECK YOUR EMAIL

You probably have hundreds, if not thousands, of emails you have sent or received. Or maybe you're a task-oriented person like me, who feels compelled to empty your inbox every day. Even though I keep my inbox empty, I have thousands of emails in folders. Recently, just by looking at the names on my email folders (without looking *into* any of them), I got more than a dozen ideas of people I could invite to church. I was amazed by how many Great Commission opportunities I was able to find with just a glance. Perhaps you can leverage your email files in a similar way.

I specifically looked for names of people who are local, people I could invite to my church. I also looked for names of people that I am almost certain don't attend a church. Even with those parameters, I still came away with many possibilities.

I can't wait to invite three of them today.

CHECK YOUR PHONE ADDRESS BOOK

One look in my phone's address book told me two things. First, I have a lot of contacts where I only know the other person's phone number. Second, I am really hesitant to delete contacts.

In my address book, I found the names of several people I could invite. There is a videographer who dropped out of church for reasons unknown. There is a physician who was very active in church but stopped coming after a church conflict. There is the owner of the building where my wife has her studio. And that's just scanning through names from A to F, and I probably missed a few.

What does your address book tell you? Do you have a number of possibilities in your phone contacts? Are there three you could call or text and invite right now?

Ask God to open your eyes to the people you should invite.

CHECK YOUR COWORKERS AND FELLOW STUDENTS

If you work in an office or attend school, you likely have contact with several people you could invite to church. Like a lot of people, during the pandemic I worked from home instead of my usual office suite. When the quarantine lifted, I made the decision to get an office in a coworking suite. Part of the reason was financial, but I also had a Great Commission motive.

By moving into a shared suite, I figured I would have the opportunity to get to know more people who aren't believers. I was right! It is truly a great harvest field where I work. I praise God for putting me there.

You may have coworkers who are not Christians or who don't have a church they attend. If we view the workplace as an evangelistic field, our entire perspective changes. Do you know of any coworkers you can invite to church?

If you're in school, you may know several students you could invite to church. Don't assume they'll say no. We have been surprised in our studies of the unchurched to find out how many people would love to go to church with someone if they were invited.

Who among your fellow students could you invite?

CHECK YOUR MERCHANTS

If you live someplace for a while, you will inevitably get to know some of the merchants with whom you transact business on a regular basis. The people who take care of my lawn have been with me almost fifteen years. I have been to the same dry cleaner for those same fifteen years. Occasionally

I will request a grocery delivery, and the same person always makes the deliveries because the algorithms matched us.

You likely have merchants you know well. You may not be certain whether they attend church, but it never hurts to ask, even if it turns out they are active in another church. You will never know unless you ask, and I have never known an active churchgoer to be offended when I've asked about church attendance.

Do you know merchants you could invite?

CHECK YOUR NEIGHBORS

I'm embarrassed to admit that I don't know many of my neighbors. I really have no excuse because I have lived in the same house more than fifteen years. I bet you are not as lax as I am. You probably know many of your neighbors, and you probably know many of them well.

Pray about those you know. Are there some who are not in church or who are not Christians? God may be leading you to invite them to church.

Do you know some neighbors you could invite?

A SIMPLE INVITATION

You may not need guidance on the best way to write an invitation to church via email or text. By all means, use whatever wording makes you most comfortable.

My invitations tend to be brief. Here's an example of a text I sent just a week ago:

> Hey, Kristen, I want to invite you and your husband to church this Sunday. Nellie Jo and I would love to take you both out to lunch after the service.

Kristen is a merchant I know. I haven't yet met her husband, but I hope to soon. I would have told her the name of the church, the address, and the times of the services, but I gave her a card with that information the last time I saw her. She responded by letting me know she still had the card.

Okay, it's time for you to invite your three people. Pray about it. Write the emails or texts. See what God will do.

Sign and date here when you have completed the twenty-first day of the thirty-day challenge to become a Great Commission Christian.

Name: ....

Date: ....

INVITE SOMEONE YOU DON'T KNOW

Meet the severe introvert.

People who know me only casually often find it hard to believe that I'm uncomfortable around people I don't know very well. I can be somewhat outgoing and conversational in such situations if I have to be. But the operative phrase is "if I have to be." I've learned I can be a functional extrovert at times. Because I am in public quite a bit, I can't just ignore people and stand in a corner by myself. But often that's exactly what I'd like to do.

Other than when I spend time with family and close friends, I am emotionally and physically drained after spending extended time around people I don't know or don't know well. I especially cringe when someone wants to buy me a cup of coffee and pick my brain.

I know, it's rather snobby of me to feel that way. I should do better. But that's my reality. I struggle when I am around people I don't know. But now I am asking you to write to someone you don't know.

I wonder how this assignment makes you feel. Frankly, being an introvert, it's easier for me to write a letter than to engage with someone in person.

Perhaps you're wondering who you should write to, especially when it's somebody you don't know. Let's look at some possibilities.

GUESTS WHO HAVE VISITED YOUR CHURCH IN THE PAST

I love it when churches keep records of people who have visited in the past. Obviously, there has to be some process in place to get that information. Allow me a brief excursion to help your church get more guest cards completed and returned. There are three major elements.

First, the pastor or some person with a level of authority must draw attention to the guest card during the worship service. If no one mentions it, visitors will not complete it and return it.

Second, you must ask *everyone* to complete it, members and guests alike. If most of the congregation is reaching for the card, a guest is more likely to complete it as well. That's why some churches don't call it a guest card but use a general term such as *ministry card*.

Third, many churches have found it very effective to provide an incentive for turning in the card. Our church donates five dollars to local community ministries for every card turned in during the worship services. If one hundred cards come in, the church donates five hundred dollars to the ministries.

Now, back to the matter of inviting people you don't know. Again, if your church has records of those who have visited in the past, that would be a perfect source. Try to find the name of someone who is local and not connected with the church.

In some churches, the small groups or Sunday school classes have records of previous guests. If not, some of the members of those groups will likely recall a name for you.

THE GOLD MINE OF MEMBER CONNECTIONS

Here is an almost certain way to get some names of people to write to. Send an email to a few members you know. Here is an example of an email I wrote not too long ago:

> I am writing to the three of you so I can become
> a better Great Commission Christian. Would you
> give me the names and emails of some people I
> could invite to church? These names could be your
> neighbors, coworkers, family members, or anyone

else you know. I promise I will write a simple email inviting them to church. I will use your name if you want me to. If you don't mention using your name, I will not include it in my email. I have no other motive than to invite people to church so they can be reached and ministered to with the gospel of Christ.

The names started rolling in!

I was very comfortable writing to those three church members because I know them well and because I know they trust me. You will be amazed by how many opportunities there are to reach people with the gospel or invite them to church when you start looking.

One church member jumped at providing the name of her mother. Her mom had been out of church for almost twenty years. Though the daughter had invited her mom to church more than once, the mother's response was tepid at best. But she responded positively and immediately when someone else invited her.

Indeed, this email you will write to someone you don't know could have profound and eternal consequences.

LEADERS IN THE COMMUNITY

Though you may have already written to a leader in your community in this challenge, there is absolutely nothing wrong with writing to other leaders. Here is a possible way to find someone. Look at a recent issue of your local paper or newsletter. Most communities have at least a digital version that comes out on a regular basis.

See if you can find a story about a leader. Perhaps a county commissioner is planning to introduce an initiative to create a small park in the community. You could write to thank her for her efforts and invite her to church in the same email. This approach has been effective in a number of churches.

It's really not hard to find the names and locate the emails of community leaders. It's usually a matter of public record. Inevitably, the leader will write back and thank you for your encouragement. And he or she just might show up at your church. That's the Great Commission in action!

IF ALL ELSE FAILS . . .

I don't imagine you'll have any trouble finding someone you don't already know to write to. I am quite certain you have ideas beyond those I've suggested. But if you still haven't come up with a single name, then invite someone you know. It could be someone who hasn't been in your small group or Sunday school class in a while. It could be a merchant to whom you've written before. It could be a family member who is only an occasional church attender.

The main purpose of these daily challenges is to get you

looking beyond yourself. On many of the days, you've prayed for specific areas in your life, your church, and your community. On other days, you've studied Bible verses to move you toward an outward focus.

The purpose of today's challenge is simply to get you thinking about someone who needs Christ, or at the very least needs a church home.

So, if you still can't come up with a name, pray that God will bring someone to mind. Though this challenge is to write to someone you don't know, don't worry if you can only think of someone who is an acquaintance or a friend.

Though I should never be surprised at how God works, I am still amazed at how he can use a simple email to change the path of someone's eternity. Now that you have a name and contact information, write a note to that person. Email him or her right now. Don't let the moment pass.

God could indeed be using you to impact someone eternally.

Sign and date here when you have completed the twenty-second day of the thirty-day challenge to become a Great Commission Christian.

Name: ....

Date: ....

THE GREAT COMMISSION AND YOUR FAMILY

We will take a slightly different path today. Throughout this thirty-day challenge, you have been praying for a number of people, many of whom are not Christians or do not have a church home. For Day 23 we will focus on your family. But we will not just focus on the lost and unchurched in your family; we will focus on all your family members.

The apostle Paul wrote these words to his protégé Timothy: "If a man cannot manage his own household, how can he take care of God's church?" (1 Timothy 3:5). This admonition is specifically for church leaders in the context of a local congregation. But the broader application is the importance of our family in ministry. Or another way of stating it is the importance of making family our first priority of ministry.

In other words, our Great Commission ministry will not be as effective if we are neglecting our own families.

With that in mind, take time to pray for several people in your family. I will provide you a guide, but you may find yourself led in other ways to pray for your family.

PRAY FOR FAMILY MEMBERS WHO ARE CHRISTIANS

Yes, our thirty-day challenge is largely about reaching those who are not believers in Christ. Still, it is important to pray also for our family members who are Christians. Like any Christian, they have struggles. They are attacked by the evil one. Christians have money problems, family problems, work problems, and health problems. Just because they are Christians doesn't mean they don't have challenges in life.

What names come to your mind immediately? Your spouse? Your parents? Your children? Your brother? Your sister?

Specifically pray for your Christian family members to be Great Commission Christians as you are striving to be. Their lives will never be complete until they obey the Lord who commands them to go into the harvest fields. Again, you may have one of your family members specifically in mind. Or there might be several you know who need some intercessory prayer.

Pray for your Christian family members.

PRAY FOR YOUR FAMILY MEMBERS
WHO ARE NOT CHRISTIANS

It was one of those unforgettable celebratory moments. The story happened many years ago, but the joy is palpable today. I was pastoring a church in Florida. A couple in their mid-forties visited the church, and I asked for the opportunity to visit them in their home. I can still remember how the waterfront house stunned me with its beauty and view.

The Holy Spirit had obviously been moving in both of their lives. Such is the reason they visited our church. Such is the reason they welcomed a visit from me. It took only a few minutes for the husband to get to the point.

"Pastor," he began. "We have all this." He waved his hand toward the expansive water view of his home. "But we are still so empty inside. What do we need to do?"

Of course, the answer was obvious. The couple became believers in Christ that night. Then they told me about their two young adult children.

The wife spoke firmly. "We have a grown son and daughter," she said. "I think we need to talk with them about Jesus. They need him just like we do."

I smiled. These two had been Christians for only about ten minutes and they were ready to share their faith with their children.

About two weeks later, the wife called me with breathless

excitement. She and her husband had told their adult children what Christ had done for them, and both kids had become followers of Christ! It was absolutely amazing. Shortly thereafter, I baptized four people all from the same family. It was one of those moments in life and ministry I will never forget.

Do you have family members who are not Christians? Without question, it is a burden you carry. You undoubtedly have been praying for them for some time. Though I don't know you personally, I join you in praying for them right now.

PRAY FOR YOUR FAMILY MEMBERS WHO ARE GOING THROUGH DIFFICULTIES

Like you, I've had a number of challenges in life. But I hurt the most when one of my family members goes through challenges. When my wife had cancer. When one of my sons lost his job. When my youngest son lost his son. When my children or grandchildren have had challenges. I hurt the most when they hurt.

You may have family members going through pain and heartache right now. If not now, you have seen them walk paths of struggles in the past.

Think of your family members going through struggles. You probably don't have to think too hard.

Pray for them. You love them. And God does too.

PRAY FOR YOUR FAMILY MEMBERS WHO ARE DIFFICULT

Not only do family members go through difficulties, but they can also be difficult themselves. My wife and I ministered to and prayed for a woman who had continuous difficulties with her family. Her father had abandoned her at a young age. Her mother was constantly critical of her both as a child and as an adult. Her first marriage was to an abusive husband.

And though her second husband is a godly man who loves and respects his wife, our friend still deals with the aftermath of her first horrendous marriage. Her children from the first marriage carry a lot of resentment, and they often take it out on our friend. And one of her children has already been in a bad marriage herself—now divorced and fighting custody issues.

We pray for her because we know her family pain causes a deep pain for her. You might be dealing with difficult family members. Perhaps you are not reconciled to a family member despite your best, prayerful efforts.

Pray for those family members who are distant from you. Pray for them even when they take out their problems on you.

PRAY FOR YOURSELF AS A FAMILY MEMBER

You can only become an effective Great Commission family member if you show the love of Christ in your relationships. I watched my late father live out his faith with family members, many of whom were difficult and presented great challenges. I saw him love a sibling who was not kind to him. I saw him take care of his alcoholic father, who seemed perpetually in a drunken state. I saw him love my mother unconditionally with a total servant spirit.

And I saw him love me despite my rebellious youth years. I saw him stand by me when I was suspended from high school. He never excused my actions, but he never wavered in his love and support for me.

I guess my dad was one of the most powerful Great Commission Christians I have ever known, primarily because he demonstrated that love to his family again and again.

Though I was led to Christ by my high school football coach, I really think my greatest influence was my dad. In my earthly father I clearly saw my heavenly Father.

Like my dad, I pray I can be a Great Commission Christian to my family members.

Would you join me in that prayer for yourself?

Sign and date here when you have completed the twenty-third day of the thirty-day challenge to become a Great Commission Christian.

Name: ....

Date: ....

PRAYING AWAY THE OBSTACLES

I can make you a promise. Since you've made a commitment to become a Great Commission Christian, you will be confronted with obstacles. From a spiritual perspective, Satan doesn't want you to be evangelistic. In fact, I believe that evangelistic Christians are one of Satan's greatest fears. Great Commission Christians are on a mission to populate heaven and depopulate hell.

From a human perspective, life gets in the way. Messed up priorities cause us to spend less time with our family, neglect reading the Bible, stop attending church regularly, and of course stop sharing our faith.

Let's take Day 24 as a day to pray away these obstacles.

And let's also pray that God will remind us to pray away these obstacles on a regular basis.

BUSYNESS

Do you know anyone who would say they're not busy? I can't remember the last time I heard anyone say that life is slow and they have plenty of time. To the contrary, the busy life is the normal life today. And that really is sad.

Let me tell you the story of a Christian friend of mine. Ben insisted he had no margin in his life. Yes, he knew he should take time to share the gospel with others. Because he is a friend, I rather boldly asked him to look at his smartphone to see how much time he had spent on it in the recent past.

He went to Screen Time and was shocked to see these weekly averages:

Social media: 5 hours 32 minutes

Games: 2 hours 41 minutes

I asked him if he looked at social media on his laptop, and he responded sheepishly, "Yes, probably thirty minutes a day." That's another two hours and thirty minutes per week. Do you get the picture? Ben was spending eight hours a week on social media and almost three hours a week on games.

Ben turned red when I asked him if he watched television or a streaming service. He nodded affirmatively and muttered, "Yeah, a couple hours a day."

Here is Ben's *annual* time log for these three areas of his life:

Social media: 416 hours

Games: 139 hours

Television/streaming: 730 hours

Ben had 1,285 hours of *margin* per year from just these three areas! How much unrealized margin do *you* have? Though I'm not suggesting you should do away with social media or entertainment, you can certainly carve out some margin for more important aspects of your life.

Pray that you will learn God's priorities for time in your life. There is probably a lot of room for sharing the gospel.

TYRANNY OF THE URGENT

Praying away the obstacles is related to the issue of busyness. It recognizes that urgent issues will inevitably arise in our lives.

With my organization, Church Answers, I was speaking in Bradenton, Florida, for two days. Toward the end of the second day, I received a call from my youngest son, Jess.

"Dad," he said seriously, "Mom just fell and broke several bones." Nellie Jo was in Franklin, Tennessee, 740 miles from Bradenton.

Of course, I booked a flight and left the conference immediately. I was fortunate that my eldest son, Sam, was with me and could finish the speaking engagement for me. For the next two weeks, I focused on my wife during her surgery and recovery.

Urgent matters happen. They are realities of life.

Here are a couple of observations about the tyranny of the urgent. First, I hope you already have margin built into your life so you can deal with these immediate moments of need. Second, urgent matters don't have to stop evangelism. Indeed, it's possible in the midst of a crisis that you will find opportunities to be a Great Commission Christian.

Pray for wisdom when urgent matters arise. Look for gospel opportunities in them.

FEAR

I admit I haven't confirmed the number, but different sources I checked said that "Do not fear" is in the Bible 365 times. That's one admonition and encouragement for every day of the year.

God knows we have to deal with fear. It is a normal emotional reaction to many challenges in life. As an introvert, I fear going to social events where I am expected to carry on small talk with people I hardly know. As a child, I can remember fearing that something would happen to my parents.

Fear could very well be a reaction you have to sharing the

gospel with someone. The first time I told someone about Christ as a young adult, I thought my heart would beat right out of my chest! Then, the unexpected words came from my mouth in fear: "You don't want to go to hell, do you?" Oh dear.

By the way, God still used that moment of fear to bring my friend Jim to salvation in Christ. He calmly responded, "No, I don't. Can you tell me how to go to heaven?"

There you go.

Pray that God will either remove the fear or use it as you seek to become a more obedient Great Commission Christian.

DISCOURAGEMENT

Discouragement in life is as common as busyness and fear. We all have moments when we struggle with life events. When I started Church Answers, most people encouraged me. They thought it would be a great ministry. But I was surprised at the people, albeit only a few, who gave me reasons why I shouldn't start the ministry.

Unfortunately, for a week or so, I listened to the discouraging voices in my head. For that brief period, my emotions changed from enthusiasm to fear. Fortunately, I began to focus more on God's vision for Church Answers and the fear went away.

Sometimes you will be afraid at the thought of telling someone about Jesus. On other occasions you will be discouraged because of other life issues. That discouragement could prove to be a distraction from your commitment to be a Great Commission Christian.

Pray that God will protect you from letting discouragement distract you from Great Commission obedience.

EXCUSES

I wish I could say I have a good excuse when I'm negligent about sharing my faith. The issue for me is that I just don't do it.

We can try to use excuses: We're too busy. We don't know what to say. We don't have any unbelievers in our lives. We don't know how to deal with objections. We don't want to offend people. We don't want people to see us as crazy or weird.

Perhaps you've used one or more of those excuses. Or perhaps you are more like I am. You really don't have an excuse. You simply fail to be obedient at times.

I do remember several years ago thinking that my main challenge in being a Great Commission Christian was finding the time to witness. In other words, my excuse was that I was too busy. Then I started praying that God would give me opportunities to share the gospel in the midst of my busyness. Since that prayer, I have been blessed by one opportunity after another.

Ask God to work in the midst of your excuses. You will be amazed to see how he answers that prayer.

Sign and date here when you have completed the twenty-fourth day of the thirty-day challenge to become a Great Commission Christian.

Name: ....

Date: ....

GO WITH PRAYERS OF EVANGELISM

My team and I interview several church members in the context of a consultation. The focus of the interviews is pretty basic: How long have you been at the church? What areas of ministry have you been or are you involved in? What are some of the strengths of the church? What are some of the challenges of the church? Is there anything else you would like to add?

During the interviews, we welcome deeper discussions of each question. We also allow the church members to take detours off the specific questions. We often get insightful information about the church when we move off script.

In one particular church, a common response to the question about challenges in the church was "We aren't reaching people!" After a few follow-up conversations, I came to a sad realization. Most of these church members did not understand evangelism. In fact, it got to a point that I added a question to my interview template: "What is your church doing to reach people evangelistically?" Very few attempted to answer the question, because they didn't understand it. One brave seventysomething man did ask me in response: "What exactly is evangelism?"

I have discovered that many professing Christians not only do not share their faith, but they also don't understand what it means to share their faith.

I trust that *you* understand it. For twenty-five days, you have been praying, studying Scripture, and going out into your neighborhood or community. You have been praying for people in the homes along your way. You have been praying and going because you want the people in your neighborhood to know the touch of Christ for physical healing, for emotional struggles, for broken relationships, and for salvation.

You know the meaning of evangelism. You know that it means to share the Good News of Christ. You know that the only way to heaven is through Christ. In fact, Jesus said it himself: "I am the way, the truth, and the life. No one can come to the Father except through me" (John 14:6).

You are faithfully seeking to be a Great Commission

Christian. You have committed to these thirty days out of obedience to that command from Jesus.

TEN HOMES WITH A FOCUS

It's time to go to another ten homes. It's time to pray for the people in those homes. Can you believe that after today's exercise you will have prayed for thirty families in your community? Do you wonder what changes are happening in those homes? Do you wonder how God has used your prayers in those homes?

You don't need any further instructions on how this exercise works. You are a pro by now. But I'm asking that you focus your prayers on *evangelism* this time. Though you probably don't know who is or isn't a Christian in the homes you pray for, pray for each home as if there is at least one person there who is not a believer. Unfortunately, the likelihood of at least one member of the family not being a Christian is high.

If possible, focus your prayer into three brief areas. Let's look at each one in turn.

PRAY FOR THEIR SALVATION

Start your prayer for each home by praying for the salvation of each person inside who is not a Christian. Pray that the Holy Spirit would convict them of their sins and that they would repent and place their faith in Christ. Pray that their hearts would be receptive to salvation in Christ.

As you pray for their salvation, pray also that God will send a message or a messenger to the people in the home. Many years ago, I was praying for someone to become a Christian, but she really didn't seem interested. Sadly, after a time, I really didn't think about witnessing to her anymore.

One night she called me. She told me she had just accepted Christ. I was stunned. Then she told me she was watching an old Billy Graham crusade on television. It became clear to her that she was not a Christian, and she needed to follow Christ immediately.

I never cease to be amazed how God uses messengers. It could be an evangelist on TV. It could be a verse of Scripture that someone stumbles across. It could be a casual conversation with someone. As you pray for the salvation of those in each of the ten homes, ask God to send them a message or a messenger.

PRAY TO REMOVE OBSTACLES

You took time yesterday, on Day 24, to pray that God would remove obstacles in your life that are hindering you from becoming a Great Commission Christian. Take a few seconds at each home to pray that obstacles to the gospel will be removed for those who have not yet become Christians.

The ways that someone could be hindered from hearing the gospel are numerous. We might think that the obstacles would be difficulties and challenges they are facing. But even more likely, people are hindered from the gospel because they're comfortable. They don't want anything to get in the way of their life or lifestyle.

Such is the story of the rich man (sometimes called the rich young ruler) and Jesus. He had a good life, and he was a moral man. When he wanted to know how to receive eternal life, Jesus told him to sell all his possessions. Jesus realized that the man's wealth was an obstacle to the gospel. You know how this part of the story ends: "But when the young man heard this, he went away sad, for he had many possessions" (Matthew 19:22).

Jesus then reminded his disciples how comfort and possessions can be an obstacle to the gospel: "I tell you the truth, it is very hard for a rich person to enter the Kingdom of Heaven. I'll say it again—it is easier for a camel to go through the eye of a needle than for a rich person to enter the Kingdom of God!" (Matthew 19:23-24).

Pray for obstacles to the gospel to be removed—especially the obstacles of comfort and possessions.

PRAY FOR THEM TO FIND A CHURCH

I am continually encouraged to hear stories of people visiting a church and then becoming Christians. Some hear the gospel in the pastor's sermons. Some through relationships they develop with other believers. These relationships become pathways to the gospel.

Some people have said they had no joy or fulfillment in their lives until they connected with a church. There they saw normal people, with problems like anyone else, living joyful and fulfilled lives. In the words of a friend who is a recent convert to Christianity at my church, "They dealt with the same mess I had to deal with, but they had joy anyway." He saw the gospel lived out in the lives of Christians in the community called the local church. He wanted what they had.

While church attendance alone won't turn an unbeliever into a Christian, church gatherings are a place where they will hear the gospel and see the gospel lived out. Perhaps God will use your prayer that people will find a church as an instrument toward their salvation.

Now it's time to go. It's time to pray for ten more families. I have already prayed for you.

Sign and date here when you have completed the twenty-fifth day of the thirty-day challenge to become a Great Commission Christian.

Name: ....

Date: ....

TELLING YOUR STORY

Anyone who has heard me speak over the past few decades may have heard me mention Coach Joe. But if you haven't heard, Coach Joe was my high school football coach and the person who led me to Christ. I usually keep the story brief, but I will add a few more details here.

I was a troubled youth. It was no fault of my parents. I was blessed to grow up in a loving and happy home. Frankly, the more I have reflected on my youth, the more I see that my rebellion was simply a product of my sinful nature. I could point to a time in high school when a teacher had some other students beat me up several times while he watched, because I wouldn't go out for a team he coached. Yes, it was traumatic, but if I'm honest with myself, I know that my rebellion preceded those events.

I dropped out of church when I was twelve. My parents probably should have pushed me more to get back in, but, again, it was really no one's fault but my own.

I found a great outlet in high school football. I wasn't a superstar, but I wasn't bad either. And it was on my first football team that I met Coach Joe Hendrickson. He called me into his office one day and just started sharing the gospel with me. I still recall how natural it was for him.

He told me how all have sinned and fallen short of the glory of God. He told me that no one can get to heaven outside of Jesus Christ. He told me how to repent and place my faith in Christ. Though his words were serious and heartfelt, they were also calm and assuring.

That night I made a decision. I repented of my sins and trusted Christ to be my Savior. I was born again.

That's it. That's my story.

Over the years as I have told my story, I often add specific verses, such as Romans 3:23 and John 14:6. If time allows, I might go into more detail about my rebellious years and my relationship with Coach Joe. But I can also tell an abbreviated version of my story in a couple of minutes.

I have been gratified by how many people remember my story. I give glory to God for those who heard my story and became followers of Christ.

I give thanks to God for saving me and for giving me a story. It's all about him.

THE POWER OF YOUR STORY

If you are a believer in Christ, you have a story. Here on Day 26, the action step is for you to put together the elements of your story. Don't be intimidated by the process. Most of the time when someone asks us to tell them something about ourselves, we talk about our family or our vocation. We should also be ready to tell our spiritual story. We must be ready to explain how we came to faith in Jesus.

First, recall a time when you were not a believer. In a recent conversation with my son Jess, I asked him about his story. He became a Christian at a young age, something that is not unusual when you grow up in a Christian home. But he remembered a time when he realized that he had done something in rebellion against God. He knew he was a sinner, though he may not have articulated it that way.

Second, Jess has only vague memories of a schoolteacher sharing the gospel with him. Nellie Jo and I have to remind him of the teacher's name. He also remembers praying a prayer of repentance and placing his faith in Christ. Even though the details are vague, it's his story. Though he believes beyond any doubt that he became a believer then, he has learned more deeply about what it means to follow Christ as he has grown in spiritual maturity.

I have heard dramatic stories of rebellion and salvation that are nothing like Jess's story. I have listened to people who committed horrendous crimes, who were addicted to drugs almost to the point of death, and who had multiple failed marriages. Their stories have more drama. They are clearer to recall. Those are their stories.

Can you articulate how you heard the gospel? If someone asks, will you be able to share with someone how you moved from an unrepentant sinner to a child of God? What is your story?

If you have not already done so, start putting your salvation story together. Write it in outline form or write it verbatim if that helps. Just be ready to share your story. God will give you the opportunity to tell it.

WRAPPING OUR MINDS AROUND 1 PETER 3:15

Peter wrote a letter to believers to prepare them for adversity and even persecution. He told them not to worry or be afraid about the threats they might face. Then he wrote these words: "Instead, you must worship Christ as Lord of your life. And if someone asks about your hope as a believer, always be ready to explain it" (1 Peter 3:15).

First, Peter told the church to remain focused on Christ and to make their lives holy. Second, when others see that your life is different and kind and loving, be ready to explain why you do what you do and why you say what you say.

In other words, be ready to tell your story.

I love the three major parts of that single verse. It is first an admonition to live a holy life so that others will see Christ in us. It's not a life of perfection, but a life that seeks to be closer to Jesus. Next, Peter tells us to be expectant that people would ask us about our faith. Jesus makes it clear in Matthew 9:37-38 that there is a huge harvest field waiting for people like you who will gladly tell their story.

Finally, Peter tells us we must have our story ready: "Always be ready to explain it." Those words are powerful. It is one of those Great Commission imperatives that is often overlooked. Yes, we are to make disciples. Yes, we are to go into the harvest fields. And yes, we must always be ready to explain where and how we gained our hope as believers.

By the way, Peter rightly presumes that others will ask us about our hope in Christ. We need to understand his words clearly. If we walk with Christ, and if we make ourselves available to share the Good News with others, God will put people in our paths.

As you grow as a Great Commission Christian, you will be amazed at how many times you have an opportunity to share the gospel and tell your story. Most people love to hear a good story. You have the greatest story. You once were blind, but now you see. You once were lost, but now you are found.

Get ready to tell your story. Countless people are waiting.

I have already prayed for you.

Sign and date here when you have completed the twenty-sixth day of the thirty-day challenge to become a Great Commission Christian.

Name: ....

Date: ....

RECONCILIATION AND THE GREAT COMMISSION

The Great Commission.

We have seen those three words a lot in this book. In fact, we have modified it a bit at times to reflect our goal for these thirty days: becoming a Great Commission Christian.

Let's look a bit more deeply into the two primary words. A *commission* is an order or directive from a higher authority. It can be an assignment given to a group or an individual. Because the commission is given by someone, or some group, in authority, the person carrying out the commission has the same authority.

Of course, we know the authority for the Great Commission comes from Jesus. He reminds us of that reality in Matthew 28:18: "I have been given all authority in heaven and on earth." Immediately after he says those words, he proclaims, "Therefore, go . . ." (Matthew 28:19). Clearly, we are to go under the authority of Christ, who commissions us.

Throughout the history of the church, we have attached the superlative *great* to this commission from our Lord and Savior. In other words, we see this particular command from Jesus as one of utmost importance. We have already noted that the words of Acts 1:8 were Jesus' last words before he ascended to heaven. It was his "last will and testament" to us. It was truly a commission of great importance.

Our obedient response to the Great Commission is an act of worship. We have said *yes* to the King of kings. We are ready to go.

Unless . . .

We are unreconciled to someone.

UNDERSTANDING MATTHEW 5:23-24

When Matthew wrote his gospel, he knew that many Jews would be among the primary audience. And he knew that the Jews understood well the sacrificial system of their day. When a sacrifice was brought to the Temple, it was an act of profound worship and service to God.

I wonder if these words from Matthew 5:23-24 struck the audience with their obvious profundity: "If you are presenting a sacrifice at the altar in the Temple and you suddenly remember that someone has something against you, leave your sacrifice there at the altar. Go and be reconciled to that person. Then come and offer your sacrifice to God."

Jesus' words are abundantly clear. You can't get your relationship straight with God until your relationships are good with others. So Jesus told them not to come into the Temple if they had a broken relationship with someone.

For those of us desiring to become Great Commission Christians, we are reminded that we cannot serve God well if we have other relationships that need mending. What does that mean for us?

PERSONALLY RECONCILE WITH PEOPLE WHERE POSSIBLE

The key word here is *personally*. Can you meet with them in person? Can you connect on one of the many meeting platforms now available? Can you call them on the phone? Are there ways you can reach out personally to anyone with whom you've had a breach of relationship? Though written communication is not always as good as meeting in person or calling someone, it might be a path for you to take.

Do you have a story of reconciliation? Ed Stetzer and

I have made public our story about the enmity between us that was followed by reconciliation. He and I have very different personalities, and those differences were magnified when we worked together at a seminary. Our dislike for one another turned into a shouting match on one occasion. There were many tense moments during those years.

A few years later, Ed reached out to me. I give him full credit for initiating the reconciliation in our relationship. If I recall correctly, he first contacted me by email to compliment me on something I had written. We had different types of communication from that point forward. We later worked together again in another organization. I doubt that either of us would have predicted that outcome.

Ed and I still have the same different personalities. And there have been moments of disagreement since our reconciliation. But disagreements do not and should not lead to estrangement. I see now more clearly the gifts and abilities Ed has. It has been good to focus on them more than our differences.

AT THE VERY LEAST, RECONCILE IN PRINCIPLE

In a conversation I had with a friend I'll call Jeff, he told me about the difficult relationship he'd had with his dad. Jeff had early memories of his dad telling him that he would never amount to anything. Every time Jeff tried to do something to please him, his father would tell him what he did wrong. My friend's entire childhood was shaped negatively by a parent he could never please.

His father essentially disowned his grown son when he decided to leave the family business to pursue a calling to ministry. Jeff's dad told him that if he left the company, he never wanted to see him again. Jeff was brokenhearted, but he pursued his calling anyway.

Jeff attempted to reach out to his dad a few times over the next three years. He finally gave up when his dad refused to take his calls. Four years later, Jeff's father died of a sudden heart attack.

When I called Jeff, he told me he was dealing with both grief and deep regret. He wished he had made a greater effort to reconcile with his dad. On the one hand, he knew he had made several efforts to connect with him. On the other hand, he thought he could have done more.

He could not have imagined his dad would die so young.

Jeff took a step that seems to be instructive. He reconciled with his dad in his heart. He actually verbalized a full apology with a plea for reconciliation. Through flowing tears, he spoke as if his dad were present. Though it wasn't the same as if his father had been there in person, Jeff knew that he meant what he said from the heart.

LEAVE YOUR SACRIFICE AT THE ALTAR

You have done well. You are nearing the end of your thirty-day challenge to become a Great Commission Christian. That is your "sacrifice at the altar." It is your act of obedience to a holy God.

Now, before the thirty days conclude, take time to pray about anyone with whom you are not reconciled. If any faces or names come to mind, ask God to give you a heart or willingness to reach out to that person. You might be able to make a phone call right now. Or perhaps you can start the process with an email or note encouraging this person or noting something good they have done.

You might be in the same situation that Jeff was. The person with whom you need to reconcile is no longer alive. You can't go to them personally, but you can still reconcile with them in your heart. I know. They might have hurt you deeply. Only God can give you the grace and strength to be willing to forgive them.

Jeff asked God for that same grace and strength. He knew he could not forgive his dad in his own power. But he also knew the Holy Spirit could do that work through him.

It's time to leave your sacrifice at the altar. It's time to go and be reconciled.

Sign and date here when you have completed the twenty-seventh day of the thirty-day challenge to become a Great Commission Christian.

Name: ....

Date: ....

INVITE THREE PEOPLE AGAIN

You have already invited people to church during this thirty-day challenge. It's time to do it again. The Day 28 challenge is to invite three people from your community to church. Inviting three people personally in one day might be difficult, so it's okay to email them if you can't invite them in person. But you need a plan.

Actually, the plan is very simple. We call it the "thank and invite" plan. Identify three people in your community to invite to church. I am doing the same exercise today as I write this chapter.

As I've mentioned, I live in Franklin, Tennessee, which is on the southern end of the greater Nashville area. I have lived here for almost twenty years, and I love my hometown more with each passing year. God has opened many doors for me to share the gospel in Franklin. Like any place, responses have been mixed, but no one has been antagonistic toward me.

What I'm suggesting is that you invite a government leader, a business leader, and a local merchant to your church. Here are some ideas for how to proceed.

INVITING A LOCAL GOVERNMENT LEADER

I know the names of some of our civic leaders in Franklin, but I admit that I don't know them well. So I started my search on the city's website, franklintn.gov, which I found with a simple online search. Franklin is governed by a mayor and eight aldermen, so I decided to write to the one who represents the ward where my home is located. Here is the template for my email:

Dear Alderman _____,

Thank you for your work as an alderman in Franklin. I appreciate the hours you give to our town. I know it is a big commitment of time and a labor of love on your part.

I want you to know I prayed for you specifically
today. If you ever get a chance to visit my church,
[name of the church], I would love to meet you and
your family in person.

Thank you again for all that you do for our
community. I do not take you or your work for
granted.

It took me about five minutes to look up my alderman's
name and send him the email.

By the way, people in positions of leadership typically
hear from the critics and the naysayers. Your positive email
will stand out as a source of encouragement.

INVITING A BUSINESS LEADER

Franklin, Tennessee, is a rapidly growing area. As the popula-
tion increases, new businesses are popping up all the time. A
local developer has been at the center of this growth for the
past twenty years. They have worked well with the leaders of
Franklin to maintain a balance between preserving the city's
history and moving toward the future. It seemed like a good
organization, so I decided to write to the company's CEO
and invite her to my church.

Dear Ms. _____,

Thank you for the many contributions [company name] has made to Franklin. I have watched you and your company show respect for our town while moving us forward. You have placed the good of the community before your own profits. It has not gone unnoticed.

I want you to know I prayed for you specifically today. If you ever get a chance to visit my church, [name of the church], I would love to meet you and your family in person.

Thank you again for all that you do for our community. I do not take you or your work for granted.

Again, it was easy to find her contact information on the company's website. It took me about five minutes to look her up and send the email.

INVITING A MERCHANT

As I've mentioned, when Nellie Jo and I moved to Franklin, we had to arrange for private garbage service. I asked our realtor and two neighbors for referrals, and they all enthusi-astically recommended the same company. Our realtor said that almost every home they sold ended up going with this company.

She also told us that the company was a "mom and pop" organization. Indeed, as I got to know the own-ers, they told me they were the third generation to own the company, which had been founded by the husband's grandfather.

Writing to them was easy for me because I've spoken to the owners several times over the years. Because the wife is the one who runs the office, I sent the email to her.

Dear _____,

I just wanted to thank you again for the great service you and _____ provide through [name of company]. I have lived in a number of places, and I have never had such a good waste disposal service. It is obvious that you care for your customers and that you love the city of Franklin.

I want you to know I prayed for you specifically today. If you and _____ ever get a chance to visit my church, [name of the church], I would love to meet all of your family.

Thank you again for all that you do for our community. I do not take you or your work for granted.

This company does not have a website, but I got their contact information from their social media page. The entire process took less than ten minutes.

THREE AND DONE

That's it. In less than half an hour, I was able to get the information I needed on three community leaders in my hometown, express my appreciation to them in an email, and invite them to church. It was so simple, but it could make an eternal difference.

By the way, all three recipients responded. They were all thankful that I had taken the time to contact them. Their gratitude seemed sincere. Two of them said they might visit my church in the future. The third recipient is active in another church but appreciated my invitation.

Now it's time for you to send your emails to three people. Encourage them. Express your appreciation for them. And invite them to church. When you finish your Day 28 challenge, you will have invited eight people to church during this thirty-day challenge. If only nineteen other church members joined you in this challenge, that would be 160 people invited to church.

As we get ready to finish the thirty-day challenge, look back at how far you've come. Think about how your attitude has changed. Anticipate that God will do a great work through your acts of obedience as a Great Commission Christian.

Sign and date here when you have completed the twenty-eighth day of the thirty-day challenge to become a Great Commission Christian.

Name: ....

Date: ....

TIME TO GO TO THIRTY

If I had suggested early in this thirty-day challenge that you should go into your neighborhood and pray for thirty homes, you might have felt overwhelmed. You might have quit the challenge right then, deeming it too difficult.

But you're a challenge veteran now. You've seen how God will prepare a path for you. And you've learned that praying for ten homes is not only possible, it's also pretty easy.

So now your challenge is to go to thirty more homes. It doesn't seem as intimidating now, does it? In fact, you can probably complete this challenge in under an hour. But what an incredible difference it will make. I get excited just thinking about how God will use you.

This time, you'll focus on a different prayer for three

groups of ten homes. For the first ten, pray for receptivity to the gospel. For the second group, pray that God will give them a desire to connect to a church. For the final ten homes, ask God to give the residents an unmistakable encounter with him. All of these prayers are connected, so God may answer your prayers in all three ways for some of the residents.

For now, let's look at the three different prayers for each group of ten homes.

RECEPTIVITY TO THE GOSPEL

In my mind's eye, I see you going to a specific neighborhood in your car, saying a prayer for God's Spirit to lead you, and then walking to ten homes.

For the first ten homes, your prayer is precise. You are praying that the residents in each home will be receptive to the gospel. Though you don't know whether the residents are Christians or not, you are assuming that at least one person in each home is not a believer.

The work of salvation is the work of the Holy Spirit convicting people of sin and their need for a Savior. You are simply praying for such conviction and for the hearts of the people to be open to the work of God.

You've heard my story; you know how Coach Joe shared the gospel with me. But God was working in my heart before I walked into Coach Joe's office. My meeting with him was the intersection of a receptive heart and an obedient bearer of the gospel.

You are praying for the residents of the first ten homes to have receptive hearts.

A DESIRE FOR CHRISTIAN COMMUNITY

Now you're ready for the second group of homes. For these ten, pray that the residents will have a desire to connect with followers of Christ. Specifically, pray for a desire in their hearts for Christian community in a local church.

Once an unbeliever gets connected to a church, he or she will likely be exposed to the gospel in both word and deed—through faithful teaching and in the lives of the gathered Christians.

My team at Church Answers has done a lot of research on people who are not connected to a local congregation. They comprise a large group of people we call *the unchurched*. In our interviews with unchurched people who are not followers of Christ, we have been encouraged to find that a majority are receptive to visiting a church. (See my book *The Unchurched Next Door* for the results of a major research project we conducted several years ago.)

In that same research, we found that only 5 percent of respondents were antagonistic toward Christians or churches. The unchurched world really is an open harvest field.

Today, you are praying specifically for these residents to have a desire to connect to a local church.

ENCOUNTERING GOD

God is all-knowing, all-powerful, and present everywhere. In that sense, he is at work everywhere all the time. "God moments" are taking place all the time in people's lives.

Your prayer for the final ten homes is that the residents will recognize a God moment in their lives. You are praying they will recognize God's work in and around them. And you are praying that this encounter with God will result in an openness to him.

What does a God moment look like? Here are two brief stories as examples.

Marvin was not a Christian, but he was not averse to Christianity. Though his parents didn't go to church, Marvin's grandparents—who were faithful churchgoers— were a major influence in his life. When Marvin's wife was pregnant with their first child, his granddad said to him three months before the child's birth, "When this baby comes into the world, I pray you will get him into a church. It's one of the most important things you can do."

Marvin was with his wife when Stephen was born. As he held his new son, he was suddenly struck by his granddad's words. Three months later, Marvin, his wife, and their son went to a church for the first time. Marvin and his wife soon became Christians.

Marvin described the birth of his son as a clear message from God. I call it a God moment.

In Dawn's case, it took some tragic events for her to see the need for something more in her life. First, she went through a divorce. And then six weeks later, she was in a near-fatal traffic accident. Though she survived, she was in the hospital for several weeks, followed by extensive rehab. Dawn described her moments in the hospital as a wake-up call. I would call it a God moment.

Fortunately, some members of a church near Dawn's home reached out to her while she was hospitalized. She later became a Christian and got involved in a church.

Obviously, we don't want to pray for a tragedy in someone's life to be a wake-up call or a God moment. But God does work in the depths of our despair and on the mountaintops of our joy.

Pray for a God moment for the residents of your third group of ten homes.

THE GREAT COMMISSION TO SIXTY HOMES

Can you believe that you have responded to the Great Commission by going to sixty homes? Would you ever have expected that you would accomplish such a mission in less than a month?

You have been obedient to the Great Commission command to *go*. Your goal was to pray for the residents of sixty homes, and perhaps you've had an opportunity to meet some of these people along the way. Maybe their encounter with you was part of their God moment. But whether it was through your prayers or through conversations, you have made a difference that can only be measured in the scope of eternity.

One more day to go! Let's get ready to move to the final day. As you will see, I hope and pray that this ending will actually become a new beginning.

Sign and date here when you have completed the twenty-ninth day of the thirty-day challenge to become a Great Commission Christian.

Name: ....

Date: ....

THE END IS BUT THE BEGINNING

You've done it!

You've made it to the final day of your thirty-day challenge. Let's review some of your accomplishments:

- You prayed for fifteen days specifically for areas to make you a more effective Great Commission Christian.
- You delved into five Bible passages that encouraged you toward the Great Commission.
- You obeyed the command to *go* to sixty homes and pray for the residents.
- You wrote five letters or emails of encouragement.

- You asked God to heal any broken relationships in your life.
- You invited eight people to your church.

Look at that list. Look at what you have accomplished. Look at what God has accomplished.

Now, let's wrap up this Great Commission challenge with prayers for God's continued work in your life. You have come so far. Ask God to continue his work in your life to make you a Great Commission Christian.

PRAY FOR THOSE WHO RECEIVED YOUR LETTERS OR EMAILS

God has already been working through the letters, emails, or texts you've sent. Some may have included words of encouragement. Some may have expressed your desire to let the recipients know how you have prayed for them. All have been God-sent messages.

Earlier I mentioned a text I sent to a friend whose wife is in late-stage dementia and no longer recognizes her husband. He has always been an incredible supporter of hers. He loves her dearly. He hurts deeply.

When I sent my friend a text of prayer, support, and encouragement, he responded almost immediately. "Thanks, Thom. I needed this touch just now."

I now pray for my friend more diligently.

PRAY FOR THE RESIDENTS OF THE HOMES

Over the past month, you have walked to or driven by sixty homes and prayed for the residents. If we assume an average of four people in each home, you prayed for 240 people as you walked by their homes. That is incredible!

Can you imagine the needs, the pain, the hope, and the challenges present in each home? Do you wonder how many of those residents are not Christians? Do you wonder how many are not in a church?

Here is what is likely happening in your life right now. When you drive or walk by those homes, you think of the people inside differently. You realize at a deeper level that those houses represent real people with real needs. You have greater compassion for them. You have a greater desire for them to know Christ.

You might not find out on this side of heaven the difference your prayers made. But maybe you will somehow make the connection. Remember the story of the person who was able to figure out that a new believer in his church lived in one of the homes where he had prayed? You might make that type of connection. You might not. But you can be assured that God is working through your prayers.

Take time again to pray for the people in those homes.

PRAY FOR YOUR OWN HEART AND ACTIONS

This thirty-day challenge has had a number of prayerful goals. Certainly, it is your desire to see those people become followers of Christ. You want for others to be healed physically and emotionally. You prayed for specific challenges they may be facing, even though you likely don't know the details.

But the primary purpose of this challenge was to move you toward becoming a more effective Great Commission Christian. Sadly, most Christians do not share the gospel. Far too many ignore or disobey the commands of Christ to be his witnesses.

I admit that I often yield to the sin of busyness. I know the facts of the Great Commission. I know that I am supposed to be about the work of witnessing and making disciples for Jesus. I know that every Christian has received this command. And I know that Christ has given me everything I need, all of his power and authority, to be his witness.

But too often I get too busy for my own good. My priorities get mixed up; they are not always God's priorities. I do some good things, but I don't always do the great things God has called me to do, particularly the Great Commission.

Do you identify with any of my struggles? If so, pray for yourself right now. Pray that you will give priority to those things that are God's priorities. Pray that your heart will break from the things that break the heart of God.

PRAY FOR YOUR CHURCH

I hope you are active in your church. I hope you realize how important the local church is in God's plans. I hope you remember that the New Testament, from Acts to the first three chapters of Revelation, was written about and to local churches and local church leaders. If most of the New Testament is about the local church, it must be important.

Take time today to pray for your church. I hope others in your church joined you in this Great Commission challenge. Imagine what could happen in your church if twenty members took this challenge twice a year. Those members would *go* and *pray* for 2,400 homes in a year. Think of the possibilities. Even more, pray about God's possibilities.

As a reminder, you don't have to wait for your pastor to start this Great Commission challenge. If you are in a small group or Sunday school class, you and your peers can take the challenge at least once a year. Think how that could change your church.

Above all, pray for your church. Pray for your pastor. Pray for the volunteers and staff. Pray that your church would be a Great Commission force in your community. And pray that the community would be open as members from your church engage them with the gospel.

THE END THAT BECOMES THE BEGINNING

You have done well. I mean it. You have done really well. You have persevered and taken this challenge in God's power. You truly have Great Commission grit.

Yes, it is the end of the thirty-day challenge. But I hope you will come back to it again and again. I hope you will sign and date every day of the challenge multiple times.

The Great Commission is not just another program in the church or another activity for you to check off. It is a command from Jesus, and it should be a way of life for all believers.

You have been asked to pray for many people in the course of these thirty days. Now I am going to pray for you directly from Scripture. Look closely at the words I am praying. They are the prayer of my heart:

I pray that your love will overflow more and more, and that you will keep on growing in knowledge and understanding. For I want you to understand what really matters, so that you may live pure and blameless lives until the day of Christ's return. May you always be filled with the fruit of your salvation—the righteous character produced in your life by Jesus Christ—for this will bring much glory and praise to God.

PHILIPPIANS 1:9-11

Sign and date here when you have completed the thirtieth day of the thirty-day challenge to become a Great Commission Christian.

Name: ....

Date: ....

NOTES

1. For more information about the Pray & Go video program, see PrayAndGoChurch.com.
2. "Hero Trooper Speaks Out: 'I Was the Last Officer,'" WBALTV11, March 10, 2022, www.wbaltv.com/article/hero-trooper-trooper-toni -schuck-speaks-out/39398912#.

ABOUT THE AUTHOR

Thom S. Rainer is founder and CEO of Church Answers. With nearly forty years of ministry experience, Thom has spent a lifetime committed to the growth and health of the local church and its leaders. Prior to founding Church Answers, he served as president and CEO of Lifeway Christian Resources.

Before Lifeway, he served at The Southern Baptist Theological Seminary for twelve years, where he was the founding dean of the Billy Graham School of Missions, Evangelism, and Ministry. For more than a decade, he served as pastor of four churches. He is a 1977 graduate of the University of Alabama and earned his master of divinity and PhD from The Southern Baptist Theological Seminary.

In addition to speaking in hundreds of venues over the past thirty years, Thom led the Rainer Group, a church and denominational consulting firm that provided church health insights to more than five hundred churches and other organizations from 1990 to 2005. Thom is the author of more than thirty books. He and his wife, Nellie Jo, live in Franklin, Tennessee.

DISCOVER WHAT IT REALLY MEANS TO BE A CHRISTIAN

Pastor, author, and church consultant Thom Rainer explains how you can find your true purpose within the community of fellow believers at your local church.

I Am a Christian: What does it really mean to be a Christian? In a world where everything from sports to politics, social media to podcasts, and movies to television competes for our attention, we need to get back to what is essential. When we finally grasp who we are in Christ and what our participation means to the local church, everything changes. Life begins to make sense. Our purpose becomes clear. Our mission through the local church is confirmed. Our hearts start longing to cooperate with God in the company of fellow believers.

I Am a Christian Participant's Guide: This eight-week guide is designed to accompany Thom Rainer's *I Am a Christian DVD Experience*. Created for group or individual use.

I Am a Christian DVD Experience: In this eight-week video experience, Thom Rainer will help you and your small group dig deeper into what it really means to be a Christian and how your life will bloom when it's rooted in the local church.

CP1787